DOVER · THRIFT · EDITIONS

Volpone

BEN JONSON

DOVER PUBLICATIONS, INC.
New York

DOVER THRIFT EDITIONS

GENERAL EDITOR: STANLEY APPELBAUM
EDITOR OF THIS VOLUME: CANDACE WARD

This Dover Thrift Edition may be used in its entirety, adaptation or in any other way for theatrical productions and performances, professional and amateur, without fee, permission or acknowledgment.

Copyright

Copyright © 1994 by Dover Publications, Inc.
All rights reserved under Pan American and International Copyright Conventions.

Published in Canada by General Publishing Company, Ltd., 30 Lesmill Road, Don Mills, Toronto, Ontario.

Published in the United Kingdom by Constable and Company, Ltd., 3 The Lanchesters, 162–164 Fulham Palace Road, London W6 9ER.

Bibliographical Note

This Dover edition, first published in 1994, contains the unabridged text of *Volpone; or, The Fox* as published in *The Chief Elizabethan Dramatists, Excluding Shakespeare*, Houghton Mifflin Company (The Riverside Press), Cambridge, MA, 1911. An introductory note and explanatory footnotes have been specially prepared for this edition.

Library of Congress Cataloging-in-Publication Data

Jonson, Ben, 1573?–1637.
    Volpone / Ben Jonson.
        p.   cm. — (Dover thrift editions)
    ISBN 0-486-28049-7 (pbk.)
    I. Title.   II. Series.
PR2622.A1   1994
822'.3 — dc20
                                                        93–42273
                                                        CIP

Manufactured in the United States of America
Dover Publications, Inc., 31 East 2nd Street, Mineola, N.Y. 11501

Note

BEN JONSON was born at Westminster in 1573. Before turning to play writing, he briefly followed his stepfather's trade of bricklaying, then served as a soldier in Flanders. By 1597, Jonson was a member of the Admiral's Company of actors, but his career was interrupted when he killed a fellow actor in a duel a year later. His first theatrical success came with *Every Man in His Humour* that same year, a play in which Shakespeare acted a part. Jonson enjoyed great success with his satires and tragedies, and during the reign of James I, he turned his talents to masques and court entertainments. From 1605 until about 1617, Jonson was the leading literary figure in London. With the death of James, however, Jonson's popularity declined as well as his theatrical successes and his health. He briefly recovered with an appointment as chronologer to the city of London, but he lost that office and abandoned his attempts to regain his previous standing in the London theater. Jonson died August 6, 1637.

Volpone; or The Fox, one of Jonson's most popular plays, was first performed in 1605 or 1606 at the Globe theater and remains one of the most biting satires on the more sordid aspects of human nature. Jonson's play is a masterpiece of types and a cynical commentary on the greed and vanity that formed a large part of the society it critiques. With the exception of Celia and Bonario, each character blindly pursues his own ends, though ultimately each receives his just deserts. Mosca (literally, "the fly") is perhaps the most intriguing character of all, a product of the client-patron relationship fostered not only by Volpone's Venetian society, but also by the English court that Jonson frequented for most of his professional life.

Contents

DRAMATIS PERSONAE[1]

VOLPONE, *a magnifico.*

MOSCA, *his parasite.*

VOLTORE, *an advocate.*

CORBACCIO, *an old gentleman.*

CORVINO, *a merchant.*

BONARIO, *son to Corbaccio.*

SIR POLITIC WOULD-BE, *a knight.*

PEREGRINE, *a gentleman traveler.*

NANO, *a dwarf.*

CASTRONE, *an eunuch.*

ANDROGYNO, *an hermaphrodite.*

GREGE (*or Mob*)

COMMENDATORI, *officers of justice.*

MERCATORI, *three merchants.*

AVOCATORI, *four magistrates.*

NOTARIO, *the register.*

LADY WOULD-BE, SIR POLITIC'S *Wife.*

CELIA, CORVINO'S *Wife.*

SERVITORI, *Servants, two* WAITING-WOMEN, *&c.*

---

1. Many of the characters' names are in Italian, and their translations are the names of animals — Volpone: fox; Mosca: fly; Voltore: vulture; Corbaccio: raven; Corvino: crow. Bonario means "good-natured"; Nano means "dwarf"; Castrone means "gelding"; and Androgyno means "man-woman," from the Greek.

THE ARGUMENT

V OLPONE, childless, rich, feigns sick, despairs,
O ffers his state to hopes of several heirs,
L ies languishing: his parasite receives
P resents of all, assures, deludes; then weaves
O ther cross plots, which ope themselves, are told.
N ew tricks for safety are sought; they thrive: when, bold,
E ach tempts th' other again, and all are sold.

PROLOGUE

Now, luck yet send us, and a little wit
   Will serve to make our play hit;
According to the palates of the season,
   Here is rhyme, not empty of reason.
This we were bid to credit from our poet,
   Whose true scope, if you would know it,
In all his poems still hath been this measure,
   To mix profit with your pleasure;
And not as some, whose throats their envy failing,
   Cry hoarsely, "All he writes is railing:"
And when his plays come forth, think they can flout them,
   With saying, he was a year about them.
To this there needs no lie, but this his creature,
   Which was two months since no feature:
And though he dares give them five lives to mend it,
   'T is known, five weeks fully penn'd it,

1

From his own hand, without a coadjutor,
   Novice, journeyman, or tutor.
Yet thus much I can give you as a token
   Of his play's worth, no eggs are broken,
Nor quaking custards with fierce teeth affrighted,
   Wherewith your rout are so delighted;
Nor hales he in a gull,[1] old ends reciting,
   To stop gaps in his loose writing;
With such a deal of monstrous and forc'd action,
   As might make Bethlem[2] a faction:
Nor made he his play for jests stol'n from each table,
   But makes jests to fit his fable;
And so presents quick comedy refin'd,
   As best critics have design'd;
The laws of time, place, persons he observeth,
   From no needful rule he swerveth.
All gall and copperas[3] from his ink he draineth,
   Only a little salt remaineth,
Wherewith he'll rub your cheeks, till, red with laughter,
   They shall look fresh a week after.

---

1. *gull*] an imposition, a trick.
2. *Bethlem*] or Bedlam, popular name for the Hospital of St. Mary of Bethlehem, the London insane asylum.
3. *copperas*] green vitriol, used in making ink.

ACT I

SCENE I. — *A room in Volpone's house*

Enter VOLPONE, MOSCA.

VOLP.   Good morning to the day; and next, my gold!
        Open the shrine, that I may see my saint.

[MOSCA *withdraws the curtain, and discovers piles of gold, plate, jewels,*
etc.]

        Hail the world's soul, and mine! More glad than is
        The teeming earth to see the long'd-for sun
        Peep through the horns of the celestial Ram,
        Am I, to view thy splendour dark'ning his;
        That lying here, amongst my other hoards,
        Show'st like a flame by night, or like the day
        Struck out of chaos, when all darkness fled
        Unto the centre.[1] O thou son of Sol,
        But brighter than thy father, let me kiss,
        With adoration, thee, and every relic
        Of sacred treasure in this blessed room.
        Well did wise poets, by thy glorious name,
        Title that age which they would have the best;
        Thou being the best of things, and far transcending
        All style of joy, in children, parents, friends,
        Or any other waking dream on earth:
        Thy looks when they to Venus did ascribe,
        They should have given her twenty thousand Cupids;
        Such are thy beauties and our loves! Dear saint,
        Riches, the dumb god, that giv'st all men tongues,

1. *centre*] center of the earth.

That canst do nought, and yet mak'st men do all things;
The price of souls; even hell, with thee to boot,
Is made worth heaven. Thou art virtue, fame,
Honour, and all things else. Who can get thee,
He shall be noble, valiant, honest, wise —

Mos.   And what he will, sir. Riches are in fortune
A greater good than wisdom is in nature.

Volp.   True, my beloved Mosca. Yet I glory
More in the cunning purchase of my wealth,
Than in the glad possession, since I gain
No common way; I use no trade, no venture;
I wound no earth with ploughshares, I fat no beasts
To feed the shambles; have no mills for iron,
Oil, corn, or men, to grind them into powder;
I blow no subtle glass, expose no ships
To threat'nings of the furrow-faced sea;
I turn no monies in the public bank,
No usure private.

Mos.   No, sir, nor devour
Soft prodigals. You shall ha' some will swallow
A melting heir as glibly as your Dutch
Will pills of butter, and ne'er purge for it;
Tear forth the fathers of poor families
Out of their beds, and coffin them alive
In some kind clasping prison, where their bones
May be forthcoming, when the flesh is rotten:
But your sweet nature doth abhor these courses;
You loathe the widow's or the orphan's tears
Should wash your pavements, or their piteous cries
Ring in your roofs, and beat the air for vengeance.

Volp.   Right, Mosca; I do loathe it.

Mos.   And, besides, sir,
You are not like the thresher that doth stand
With a huge flail, watching a heap of corn,
And, hungry, dares not taste the smallest grain,
But feeds on mallows, and such bitter herbs;
Nor like the merchant, who hath fill'd his vaults
With Romagnia, rich and Candian[2] wines,

---

2. *Romagnia . . . Candian*] Romagna is a district in Northern Italy on the Adriatic Sea; Candia is the Isle of Crete.

Yet drinks the lees of Lombard's vinegar:
You will not lie in straw, whilst moths and worms
Feed on your sumptuous hangings and soft beds;
You know the use of riches, and dare give now
From that bright heap, to me, your poor observer,
Or to your dwarf, or your hermaphrodite,
Your eunuch, or what other household trifle
Your pleasure allows maintenance —

VOL.   Hold thee, Mosca,
Take of my hand; thou strik'st on truth in all,
And they are envious term thee parasite.
Call forth my dwarf, my eunuch, and my fool,
And let 'em make me sport.   [*Exit* MOS.]
                              What should I do,
But cocker[3] up my genius, and live free
To all delights my fortune calls me to?
I have no wife, no parent, child, ally,
To give my substance to; but whom I make
Must be my heir; and this makes men observe[4] me:
This draws new clients daily to my house,
Women and men of every sex and age,
That bring me presents, send me plate, coin, jewels,
With hope that when I die (which they expect
Each greedy minute) it shall then return
Tenfold upon them; whilst some, covetous
Above the rest, seek to engross me whole,
And counter-work the one unto the other,
Contend in gifts, as they would seem in love:
All which I suffer, playing with their hopes,
And am content to coin 'em into profit,
And look upon their kindness, and take more,
And look on that; still bearing them in hand,[5]
Letting the cherry knock against their lips,
And draw it by their mouths, and back again. —
How now!

---

3. *cocker*] to pamper.
4. *observe*] pay obsequious attention to.
5. *bearing . . . hand*] deceiving them by false hopes.

SCENE II. — *The same*

To him re-enter MOSCA, *with* NANO, ANDROGYNO, *and* CASTRONE.

NAN.   "Now, room for fresh gamesters, who do will you to know,
They do bring you neither play nor university show;
And therefore do intreat you that whatsoever they rehearse,
May not fare a whit the worse, for the false pace of the verse.
If you wonder at this, you will wonder more ere we pass,
For know, here[1] is inclos'd the soul of Pythagoras,
That juggler divine, as hereafter shall follow;
Which soul, fast and loose, sir, came first from Apollo,
And was breath'd into Aethalides, Mercurius his son,
Where it had the gift to remember all that ever was done.
From thence it fled forth, and made quick transmigration
To goldy-lock'd Euphorbus, who was kill'd in good fashion,
At the siege of old Troy, by the cuckold of Sparta.
Hermotimus was next (I find it in my charta).
To whom it did pass, where no sooner it was missing,
But with one Pyrrhus of Delos it learn'd to go a-fishing;
And thence did it enter the sophist of Greece.
From Pythagore, she went into a beautiful piece,
Hight Aspasia, the meretrix; and the next toss of her
Was again of a whore, she became a philosopher,
Crates the cynick, as itself doth relate it:
Since kings, knights, and beggars, knaves, lords, and fools
     gat it,
Besides ox and ass, camel, mule, goat, and brock,[2]
In all which it hath spoke, as in the cobbler's cock.[3]
But I come not here to discourse of that matter,
Or his one, two, or three, or his great oath, BY QUATER![4]
His musics, his trigon,[5] his golden thigh,

---

1. *here*] in Androgyno.
2. *brock*] badger.
3. *cock*] This interlude is based on Lucian's dialogue between a cobbler and a cock.
4. *Quater*] quatre, the four in dice.
5. *trigon*] a triangular lyre.

	Or his telling how elements shift; but I
	Would ask, how of late thou hast suffer'd translation,
	And shifted thy coat in these days of reformation.
AND.	Like one of the reform'd, a fool, as you see,
	Counting all old doctrine heresy.
NAN.	But not on thine own forbid meats hast thou ventur'd?
AND.	On fish, when first a Carthusian I enter'd.
NAN.	Why, then thy dogmatical silence hath left thee?
AND.	Of that an obstreperous lawyer bereft me.
NAN.	O wonderful change, when sir lawyer forsook thee!
	For Pythagore's sake, what body then took thee?
AND.	A good dull mule.
NAN.	And how! by that means
	Thou wert brought to allow of the eating of beans?
AND.	Yes.
NAN.	But from the mule into whom didst thou pass?
AND.	Into a very strange beast, by some writers call'd an ass;
	By others a precise,[6] pure, illuminate brother
	Of those devour flesh, and sometimes one another;
	And will drop you forth a libel, or a sanctifi'd lie,
	Betwixt every spoonful of a nativity-pie.[7]
NAN.	Now quit thee, for heaven, of that profane nation.
	And gently report thy next transmigration.
AND.	To the same that I am.
NAN.	A creature of delight,
	And, what is more than a fool, an hermaphrodite!
	Now, prithee, sweet soul, in all thy variation,
	Which body wouldst thou choose to keep up thy station?
AND.	Troth, this I am in: even here would I tarry.
NAN.	'Cause here the delight of each sex thou canst vary?
AND.	Alas, those pleasures be stale and forsaken;
	No, 't is your fool wherewith I am so taken,
	The only one creature that I can call blessed;
	For all other forms I have prov'd most distressed.
NAN.	Spoke true, as thou wert in Pythagoras still.
	This learned opinion we celebrate will,
	Fellow eunuch, as behoves us, with all our wit and art,

6. *precise*] puritanical.
7. *nativity-pie*] Christmas-pie.

        To dignify that whereof ourselves are so great and special a
           part."

VOLP.   Now, very, very pretty! Mosca, this
        Was thy invention?

MOS.   If it please my patron,
        Not else.

VOLP.   It doth, good Mosca.

MOS.   Then it was, sir.

[NANO *and* CASTRONE *sing.*]

SONG.

"Fools, they are the only nation
Worth men's envy or admiration;
Free from care or sorrow-taking,
Selves and others merry making:
All they speak or do is sterling.
Your fool he is your great man's darling,
And your ladies' sport and pleasure;
Tongue and bauble are his treasure.
E'en his face begetteth laughter,
And he speaks truth free from slaughter;[8]
He's the grace of every feast,
And sometimes the chiefest guest;
Hath his trencher[9] and his stool,
When wit waits upon the fool.
  O, who would not be
  He, he, he?"

                                One knocks without.

VOLP.   Who's that? Away! Look, Mosca.
        Fool, begone!
                  [*Exeunt* NANO, CAST. *and* ANDRO.]

MOS.   'T is Signior Voltore, the advocate;
        I know him by his knock.

VOLP.   Fetch me my gown,
        My furs, and night-caps; say my couch is changing
        And let him entertain himself a while
        Without i' th' gallery. [*Exit* MOSCA.] Now, now my clients

---

8. *free from slaughter*] with impunity.
9. *trencher*] plate.

Begin their visitation! Vulture, kite,
Raven, and gorcrow,[10] all my birds of prey,
That think me turning carcase, now they come:
I am not for 'em yet.

[*Re-enter* MOSCA, *with the gown, etc.*]

              How now! the news?
MOS.   A piece of plate, sir.
VOLP.   Of what bigness?
MOS.   Huge,
Massy, and antique, with your name inscrib'd,
And arms engraven.
VOLP.   Good! and not a fox
Stretcht on the earth, with fine delusive sleights,
Mocking a gaping crow? ha, Mosca!
MOS.   Sharp, sir.
VOLP.   Give me my furs.

                          [*Puts on his sick dress.*]
              Why dost thou laugh so, man?
MOS.   I cannot choose, sir, when I apprehend
What thoughts he has without now, as he walks:
That this might be the last gift he should give,
That this would fetch you; if you died to-day,
And gave him all, what he should be to-morrow;
What large return would come of all his ventures;
How he should worshipp'd be, and reverenc'd;
Ride with his furs, and foot cloths; waited on
By herds of fools and clients; have clear way
Made for his mule, as letter'd as himself;
Be call'd the great and learned advocate:
And then concludes, there's nought impossible.
VOLP.   Yes, to be learned, Mosca.
MOS.   O, no: rich
Implies it. Hood an ass with reverend purple,
So you can hide his two ambitious[11] ears,
And he shall pass for a cathedral doctor.
VOLP.   My caps, my caps, good Mosca. Fetch him in.

---

10. *gorcrow*] carrion crow.
11. *ambitious*] also a reference to the word's etymological sense of "moving round."

Mos.	Stay, sir; your ointment for your eyes.
Volp.	That's true;

Dispatch, dispatch: I long to have possession
Of my new present.

Mos.   That, and thousands more,
I hope to see you lord of.

Volp.   Thanks, kind Mosca.

Mos. And that, when I am lost in blended dust,
And hundreds such as I am, in succession —

Volp. Nay, that were too much, Mosca.

Mos.   You shall live
Still to delude these harpies.

Volp.   Loving Mosca!
'T is well: my pillow now, and let him enter.

                                  [*Exit* Mosca.]

Now, my feign'd cough, my phthisic,[12] and my gout,
My apoplexy, palsy, and catarrhs,
Help, with your forced functions, this my posture,
Wherein, this three year, I have milk'd their hopes.
He comes; I hear him — Uh! [*coughing*] uh! uh! uh! O —

SCENE III. — *The same*

VOLPONE; *re-enter* MOSCA, *introducing* VOLTORE *with a piece of plate.*

Mos. You still are what you were, sir. Only you,
Of all the rest, are he commands his love,
And you do wisely to preserve it thus,
With early visitation, and kind notes
Of your good meaning to him, which, I know,
Cannot but come most grateful. Patron! sir!
Here's Signior Voltore is come —

Volp. [*Faintly.*]   What say you?

Mos. Sir, Signior Voltore is come this morning
To visit you.

---

12. *phthisic*] phthisis, a progressively wasting or consumptive condition.

VOLP.	I thank him.
MOS.	And hath brought
	A piece of antique plate, bought of St. Mark,[1]
	With which he here presents you.
VOLP.	He is welcome.
	Pray him to come more often.
MOS.	Yes.
VOLT.	What says he?
MOS.	He thanks you, and desires you see him often.
VOLP.	Mosca.
MOS.	My patron!
VOLP.	Bring him near, where is he?
	I long to feel his hand.
MOS.	The plate is here, sir.
VOLT.	How fare you, sir?
VOLP.	I thank you, Signior Voltore;
	Where is the plate? mine eyes are bad.
VOLT.	[*putting it into his hands.*] I'm sorry
	To see you still thus weak.
MOS.	[*Aside.*] That he's not weaker.
VOLP.	You are too munificent.
VOLT.	No, sir; would to heaven
	I could as well give health to you, as that plate!
VOLP.	You give, sir, what you can; I thank you. Your love
	Hath taste in this, and shall not be unanswer'd:
	I pray you see me often.
VOLT.	Yes, I shall, sir.
VOLP.	Be not far from me.
MOS.	Do you observe that, sir?
VOLP.	Hearken unto me still; it will concern you.
MOS.	You are a happy man, sir; know your good.
VOLP.	I cannot now last long —
MOS.	(*Aside.*) You are his heir, sir.
VOLT.	(*Aside.*) Am I?
VOLP.	I feel me going: Uh! uh! uh! uh!
	I'm sailing to my port. Uh! uh! uh! uh!
	And I am glad I am so near my haven.
MOS.	Alas, kind gentleman! Well, we must all go —

---

1. *bought of St. Mark*] at one of the goldsmith's shops beside St. Mark's.

VOLT.   But, Mosca—

MOS.   Age will conquer.

VOLT.   Prithee, hear me;
     Am I inscrib'd his heir for certain?

MOS.   Are you!
     I do beseech you, sir, you will vouchsafe
     To write me i' your family. All my hopes
     Depend upon your worship: I am lost
     Except the rising sun do shine on me.

VOLT.   It shall both shine, and warm thee, Mosca.

MOS.   Sir,
     I am a man that hath not done your love
     All the worst offices: here I wear your keys,
     See all your coffers and your caskets lock'd,
     Keep the poor inventory of your jewels,
     Your plate, and monies; am your steward, sir,
     Husband your goods here.

VOLT.   But am I sole heir?

MOS.   Without a partner, sir: confirm'd this morning:
     The wax is warm yet, and the ink scarce dry
     Upon the parchment.

VOLT.   Happy, happy me!
     By what good chance, sweet Mosca?

MOS.   Your desert, sir;
     I know no second cause.

VOLT.   Thy modesty
     Is loth to know it; well, we shall requite it.

MOS.   He ever lik'd your course, sir; that first took him.
     I oft have heard him say how he admir'd
     Men of your large profession, that could speak
     To every cause, and things mere contraries,
     Till they were hoarse again, yet all be law;
     That, with most quick agility, could turn,
     And return; make knots, and undo them;
     Give forked counsel; take provoking gold
     On either hand, and put it up; these men,
     He knew, would thrive with their humility.
     And, for his part, he thought he should be blest
     To have his heir of such a suff'ring spirit,
     So wise, so grave, of so perplex'd a tongue,

And loud withal, that would not wag, nor scarce
Lie still, without a fee; when every word
Your worship but lets fall, is a chequin![2] —

Another knocks.

Who's that? one knocks; I would not have you seen, sir.
And yet — pretend you came and went in haste;
I'll fashion an excuse — and, gentle sir,
When you do come to swim in golden lard,
Up to the arms in honey, that your chin
Is borne up stiff with fatness of the flood,
Think on your vassal; but remember me:
I ha' not been your worst of clients.

VOLT.   Mosca! —
MOS. When will you have your inventory brought, sir?
Or see a copy of the will? — Anon!
I'll bring them to you, sir. Away, begone,
Put business i' your face.   [*Exit* VOLTORE.]
VOLP. [*Springing up.*] Excellent Mosca!
Come hither, let me kiss thee.
MOS.   Keep you still, sir.
Here is Corbaccio.
VOLP.   Set the plate away:
The vulture's gone, and the old raven's come.

SCENE IV. — *The same*

MOSCA, VOLPONE.

MOS. Betake you to your silence, and your sleep.
Stand there and multiply. [*Putting the plate to the rest.*] Now
  we shall see
A wretch who is indeed more impotent
Than this can feign to be; yet hopes to hop
Over his grave.

---

2. *chequin*] zechin, or zecchino, an Italian gold coin.

[*Enter* CORBACCIO.]

                     Signior Corbaccio!
You're very welcome, sir.

CORB.   How does your patron?

MOS.   Troth, as he did, sir; no amends.

CORB.   What! mends he?

MOS.   No, sir: he's rather worse.

CORB.   That's well. Where is he?

MOS.   Upon his couch, sir, newly fall'n asleep.

CORB.   Does he sleep well?

MOS.   No wink, sir, all this night,
Nor yesterday; but slumbers.[1]

CORB.   Good! he should take
Some counsel of physicians: I have brought him
An opiate here, from mine own doctor.

MOS.   He will not hear of drugs.

CORB.   Why? I myself
Stood by while 't was made, saw all th' ingredients;
And know it cannot but most gently work:
My life for his, 't is but to make him sleep.

VOLP.   [*Aside.*] Ay, his last sleep, if he would take it.

MOS.   Sir,
He has no faith in physic.

CORB.   Say you, say you?

MOS.   He has no faith in physic: he does think
Most of your doctors are the greater danger,
And worse disease, t' escape. I often have
Heard him protest that your physician
Should never be his heir.

CORB.   Not I his heir?

MOS.   Not your physician, sir.

CORB.   O, no, no, no,
I do not mean it.

MOS.   No, sir, nor their fees
He cannot brook: he says they flay a man
Before they kill him.

CORB.   Right, I do conceive you.

MOS.   And then they do it by experiment;
For which the law not only doth absolve 'em,

---

1. *slumbers*] dozes.

	But gives them great reward: and he is loth
	To hire his death so.
CORB.	It is true, they kill
	With as much licence as a judge.
MOS.	Nay, more;
	For he but kills, sir, where the law condemns,
	And these can kill him too.
CORB.	Ay, or me;
	Or any man. How does his apoplex?
	Is that strong on him still?
MOS.	Most violent.
	His speech is broken, and his eyes are set,
	His face drawn longer than 't was wont—
CORB.	How! how!
	Stronger than he was wont?
MOS.	No, sir; his face
	Drawn longer than 't was wont.
CORB.	O, good!
MOS.	His mouth
	Is ever gaping, and his eyelids hang.
CORB.	Good.
MOS.	A freezing numbness stiffens all his joints,
	And makes the colour of his flesh like lead.
CORB.	'T is good.
MOS.	His pulse beats slow, and dull.
CORB.	Good symptoms still.
MOS.	And from his brain—
CORB.	Ha? How? Not from his brain?
MOS.	Yes, sir, and from his brain—
CORB.	I conceive you; good.
MOS.	Flows a cold sweat, with a continual rheum,
	Forth the resolved corners of his eyes.
CORB.	Is 't possible? Yet I am better, ha!
	How does he with the swimming of his head?
MOS.	O, sir, 't is past the scotomy;[2] he now
	Hath lost his feeling, and hath left to snort:
	You hardly can perceive him, that he breathes.
CORB.	Excellent, excellent! sure I shall outlast him:
	This makes me young again, a score of years.

2. *scotomy*] imperfect sight, with giddiness.

MOS.	I was a-coming for you, sir.
CORB.	Has he made his will?
	What has he giv'n me?
MOS.	No, sir.
CORB.	Nothing! ha?
MOS.	He has not made his will, sir.
CORB.	Oh, oh, oh!
	What then did Voltore, the lawyer, here?
MOS.	He smelt a carcase, sir, when he but heard
	My master was about his testament;
	As I did urge him to it for your good —
CORB.	He came unto him, did he? I thought so.
MOS.	Yes, and presented him this piece of plate.
CORB.	To be his heir?
MOS.	I do not know, sir.
CORB.	True:
	I know it too.
MOS.	[*Aside.*] By your own scale, sir.
CORB.	Well,
	I shall prevent him yet. See, Mosca, look,
	Here I have brought a bag of bright chequins,
	Will quite lay down his plate.
MOS.	[*taking the bag.*] Yea, marry, sir.
	This is true physic, this your sacred medicine;
	No talk of opiates to this great elixir!
CORB.	'T is *aurum palpabile*, if not *potabile*.[3]
MOS.	It shall be minister'd to him in his bowl.
CORB.	Ay, do, do, do.
MOS.	Most blessed cordial!
	This will recover him.
CORB.	Yes, do, do, do.
MOS.	I think it were not best, sir.
CORB.	What?
MOS.	To recover him.
CORB.	O, no, no, no; by no means.
MOS.	Why, sir, this
	Will work some strange effect, if he but feel it.

3. aurum palpabile . . . potabile] palpable, material gold, if not *aurum potabile*, or drink-
able gold, which was the elixir.

CORB.   'T is true, therefore forbear; I'll take my venture:.
       Give me 't again.
MOS.   At no hand: pardon me:
       You shall not do yourself that wrong, sir. I
       Will so advise you, you shall have it all.
CORB.   How?
MOS.   All, sir; 't is your right, your own; no man
       Can claim a part: 't is yours without a rival,
       Decreed by destiny.
CORB.   How, how, good Mosca?
MOS.   I'll tell you, sir. This fit he shall recover, —
CORB.   I do conceive you.
MOS.   And on first advantage
       Of his gain'd sense, will I re-importune him
       Unto the making of his testament:
       And show him this.   [*Pointing to the money.*]

CORB.   Good, good.
MOS.   'T is better yet,
       If you will hear, sir.
CORB.   Yes, with all my heart.
MOS.   Now would I counsel you, make home with speed;
       There, frame a will; whereto you shall inscribe
       My master your sole heir.
CORB.   And disinherit
       My son?
MOS.   O, sir, the better: for that colour[4]
       Shall make it much more taking.
CORB.   O, but colour?
MOS.   This will, sir, you shall send it unto me.
       Now, when I come to inforce, as I will do,
       Your cares, your watchings, and your many prayers,
       Your more than many gifts, your this day's present,
       And last, produce your will; where, without thought,
       Or least regard, unto your proper issue,
       A son so brave, and highly meriting,
       The stream of your diverted love hath thrown you
       Upon my master, and made him your heir;

---

4. *colour*] circumstance or appearance.

	He cannot be so stupid, or stone-dead,
	But out of conscience and mere gratitude —
CORB.	He must pronounce me his?
MOS.	'T is true.
CORB.	This plot
	Did I think on before.
MOS.	I do believe it.
CORB.	Do you not believe it?
MOS.	Yes, sir,
CORB.	Mine own project.
MOS.	Which, when he hath done, sir —
CORB.	Publish'd me his heir?
MOS.	And you so certain to survive him —
CORB.	Ay.
MOS.	Being so lusty a man —
CORB.	'T is true.
MOS.	Yes, sir —
CORB.	I thought on that too. See, how he should be
	The very organ to express my thoughts!
MOS.	You have not only done yourself a good —
CORB.	But multipli'd it on my son.
MOS.	'T is right, sir.
CORB.	Still, my invention.
MOS.	'Las, sir! heaven knows,
	It hath been all my study, all my care,
	(I e'en grow gray withal,) how to work things —
CORB.	I do conceive, sweet Mosca.
MOS.	You are he
	For whom I labour here.
CORB.	Ay, do, do, do:
	I'll straight about it. [*Going.*]
MOS.	[*Aside.*] Rook go with you,[5] raven!
CORB.	I know thee honest.
MOS.	You do lie, sir!
CORB.	And —
MOS.	Your knowledge is no better than your ears, sir.
CORB.	I do not doubt to be a father to thee.

5. *Rook go with you*] May you be rooked, or cheated.

MOS.   Nor I to gull my brother of his blessing.
CORB.   I may ha' my youth restor'd to me, why not?
MOS.   Your worship is a precious ass!
CORB.   What sayst thou?
MOS.   I do desire your worship to make haste, sir.
CORB.   'T is done, 't is done; I go.   [*Exit.*]
VOLP.   [*leaping from his couch.*] O, I shall burst!
        Let out my sides, let out my sides —
MOS.   Contain
        Your flux of laughter, sir: you know this hope
        Is such a bait, it covers any hook.
VOLP.   O, but thy working, and thy placing it!
        I cannot hold; good rascal, let me kiss thee:
        I never knew thee in so rare a humour.
MOS.   Alas, sir, I but do as I am taught;
        Follow your grave instructions; give them words;
        Pour oil into their ears, and send them hence.
VOLP.   'T is true, 't is true. What a rare punishment
        Is avarice to itself!
MOS.   Ay, with our help, sir.
VOLP.   So many cares, so many maladies,
        So many fears attending on old age,
        Yea, so often call'd on, as no wish
        Can be more frequent with 'em, their limbs faint,
        Their senses dull, their seeing, hearing, going,
        All dead before them; yea, their very teeth,
        Their instruments of eating, failing them:
        Yet this is reckon'd life! Nay, here was one,
        Is now gone home, that wishes to live longer!
        Feels not his gout, nor palsy; feigns himself
        Younger by scores of years, flatters his age
        With confident belying it, hopes he may
        With charms like Aeson,[6] have his youth restor'd;
        And with these thoughts so battens, as if fate
        Would be as easily cheated on as he,
        And all turns air! Who's that there, now? a third!
                              Another knocks.

---

6. *Aeson*] Jason's father, who was restored to life by the charm of Medea the witch.

Mos.	Close, to your couch again; I hear his voice.
	It is Corvino, our spruce merchant.
Volp.	[*Lies down as before.*] Dead.[7]
Mos.	Another bout, sir, with your eyes [*Anointing them*]. Who's
	there?

SCENE V. — *The same*

Mosca, Volpone. *Enter* Corvino.

Mos.	Signior Corvino! come most wish'd for! O,
	How happy were you, if you knew it, now!
Corv.	Why? what? wherein?
Mos.	The tardy hour is come, sir.
Corv.	He is not dead?
Mos.	Not dead, sir, but as good;
	He knows no man.
Corv.	How shall I do then?
Mos.	Why, sir?
Corv.	I have brought him here a pearl.
Mos.	Perhaps he has
	So much remembrance left as to know you, sir:
	He still calls on you; nothing but your name
	Is in his mouth. Is your pearl orient,[1] sir?
Corv.	Venice was never owner of the like.
Volp.	[*faintly.*] Signior Corvino!
Mos.	Hark!
Volp.	Signior Corvino.
Mos.	He calls you; step and give it him. — He's here, sir.
	And he has brought you a rich pearl.
Corv.	How do you, sir?
	Tell him it doubles the twelve carat.
Mos.	Sir,

---

7. *Dead*] "Pretend that I'm dead."

---

1. *orient*] brilliant or lustrous, and therefore precious.

	He cannot understand, his hearing's gone;
	And yet it comforts him to see you —
CORV.	Say
	I have a diamond for him, too.
MOS.	Best show 't, sir;

CORV.   Say
I have a diamond for him, too.

MOS.   Best show 't, sir;
Put it into his hand: 't is only there
He apprehends: he has his feeling yet.
See how he grasps it!

CORV.   'Las, good gentleman!
How pitiful the sight is!

MOS.   Tut, forget, sir.
The weeping of an heir should still be laughter
Under a visor.

CORV.   Why, am I his heir?

MOS.   Sir, I am sworn, I may not show the will
Till he be dead; but here has been Corbaccio,
Here has been Voltore, here were others too,
I cannot number 'em, they were so many;
All gaping here for legacies: but I,
Taking the vantage of his naming you,
Signior Corvino, Signior Corvino, took
Paper, and pen, and ink, and there I ask'd him
Whom he would have his heir! *Corvino.* Who
Should be executor? *Corvino.* And
To any question he was silent to,
I still interpreted the nods he made,
Through weakness, for consent: and sent home th' others,
Nothing bequeath'd them, but to cry and curse.

CORV.   O, my dear Mosca. (*They embrace.*) Does he not perceive us?

MOS.   No more than a blind harper. He knows no man,
No face of friend, nor name of any servant,
Who 't was that fed him last, or gave him drink:
Not those he hath begotten, or brought up,
Can he remember.

CORV.   Has he children?

MOS.   Bastards,
Some dozen, or more, that he begot on beggars,
Gypsies, and Jews, and black-moors, when he was drunk.
Knew you not that, sir? 't is the common fable,
The dwarf, the fool, the eunuch, are all his;

He's the true father of his family,
In all save me: — but he has giv'n 'em nothing.

CORV. That's well, that's well! Art sure he does not hear us?

MOS. Sure, sir! why, look you, credit your own sense.

[*Shouts in* VOLP.'S *ear.*]

The pox approach, and add to your diseases,
If it would send you hence the sooner, sir,
For your incontinence, it hath deserv'd it
Throughly and throughly, and the plague to boot! —
You may come near, sir. — Would you would once close
Those filthy eyes of yours, that flow with slime
Like two frog-pits; and those same hanging cheeks,
Cover'd with hide instead of skin — Nay, help, sir[2] —
That look like frozen dish-clouts set on end!

CORV. Or like an old smok'd wall, on which the rain
Ran down in streaks!

MOS.   Excellent, sir! speak out:
You may be louder yet; a culverin[3]
Discharged in his ear would hardly bore it.

CORV. His nose is like a common sewer, still running.

MOS. 'T is good! And what his mouth?

CORV.   A very draught.[4]

MOS. O, stop it up —

CORV.   By no means.

MOS.   Pray you, let me:
Faith I could stifle him rarely with a pillow
As well as any woman that should keep him.

CORV. Do as you will; but I'll begone.

MOS.   Be so;
It is your presence makes him last so long.

CORV. I pray you use no violence.

MOS.   No, sir! why?
Why should you be thus scrupulous, pray you, sir?

CORV. Nay, at your discretion.

MOS.   Well, good sir, be gone.

CORV. I will not trouble him now to take my pearl.

---

2. *Nay, help, sir*] said to Corvino, asking for his help in the abuse.
3. *culverin*] cannon.
4. *draught*] cesspool.

MOS.	Puh! nor your diamond. What a needless care
	Is this afflicts you? Is not all here yours?
	Am not I here, whom you have made your creature?
	That owe my being to you?
CORV.	Grateful Mosca!
	Thou art my friend, my fellow, my companion,
	My partner, and shalt share in all my fortunes.
MOS.	Excepting one.
CORV.	What's that?
MOS.	Your gallant wife, sir. [*Exit* CORV.]
	Now is he gone: we had no other means
	To shoot him hence but this.
VOLP.	My divine Mosca!
	Thou hast to-day outgone thyself. Who's there?

Another knocks.

I will be troubled with no more. Prepare
Me music, dances, banquets, all delights;
The Turk is not more sensual in his pleasures
Than will Volpone. [*Exit* MOS.] Let me see; a pearl!
A diamond! plate! chequins! Good morning's purchase.[5]
Why, this is better than rob churches, yet;
Or fat, by eating, once a month, a man—

[*Re-enter* MOSCA.]

	Who is 't?
MOS.	The beauteous Lady Would-be, sir,
	Wife to the English knight, Sir Politic Would-be,
	(This is the style, sir, is directed me,)
	Hath sent to know how you have slept to-night,
	And if you would be visited?
VOLP.	Not now:
	Some three hours hence.
MOS.	I told the squire[6] so much.
VOLP.	When I am high with mirth and wine; then then:
	'Fore heaven, I wonder at the desperate valour
	Of the bold English, that they dare let loose
	Their wives to all encounters!

5. *purchase*] booty.
6. *squire*] messenger.

Mos.   Sir, this knight
        Had not his name for nothing, he is *politic*,
        And knows, howe'er his wife affect strange airs,
        She hath not yet the face to be dishonest:
        But had she Signior Corvino's wife's face —
VOLP.   Hath she so rare a face?
Mos.   O, sir, the wonder,
        The blazing star of Italy! a wench
        Of the first year, a beauty ripe as harvest!
        Whose skin is whiter than a swan all over,
        Than silver, snow, or lilies; a soft lip,
        Would tempt you to eternity of kissing!
        And flesh that melteth in the touch to blood!
        Bright as your gold, and lovely as your gold!
VOLP.   Why had not I known this before?
Mos.   Alas, sir,
        Myself but yesterday discover'd it.
VOLP.   How might I see her?
Mos.   O, not possible;
        She's kept as warily as is your gold;
        Never does come abroad, never takes air
        But at a windore.[7] All her looks are sweet,
        As the first grapes or cherries, and are watch'd
        As near as they are.
VOLP.   I must see her.
Mos.   Sir,
        There is a guard of ten spies thick upon her,
        All his whole household; each of which is set
        Upon his fellow, and have all their charge,
        When he goes out, when he comes in, examin'd.
VOLP.   I will go see her, though but at her windore.
Mos.   In some disguise then.
VOLP.   That is true; I must
        Maintain mine own shape still the same: we'll think.
                                              [*Exeunt.*]

7. *windore*] window.

ACT II

SCENE I. — *St. Mark's Place; a retired corner before Corvino's house*

Enter SIR POLITIC WOULD-BE, *and* PEREGRINE.

SIR P.   Sir, to a wise man, all the world's his soil:
It is not Italy, nor France, nor Europe,
That must bound me, if my fates call me forth.
Yet I protest, it is no salt[1] desire
Of seeing countries, shifting a religion,
Nor any disaffection to the state
Where I was bred, and unto which I owe
My dearest plots, hath brought me out, much less
That idle, antique, stale, grey-headed project
Of knowing men's minds and manners, with Ulysses!
But a peculiar humour of my wife's
Laid for this height[2] of Venice, to observe,
To quote,[3] to learn the language, and so forth —
I hope you travel, sir, with licence?

PER.   Yes.

SIR P.   I dare the safelier converse — How long, sir,
Since you left England?

PER.   Seven weeks.

SIR P.   So lately!
You have not been with my lord ambassador?

PER.   Not yet, sir.

---

1. *salt*] frivolous.
2. *height*] latitude.
3. *To quote*] to make note of.

25

SIR P.	Pray you, what news, sir, vents our climate?
	I heard last night a most strange thing reported
	By some of my lord's followers, and I long
	To hear how 't will be seconded.
PER.	What was 't, sir?
SIR P.	Marry, sir, of a raven that should build
	In a ship royal of the king's.
PER.	[*Aside.*] This fellow,
	Does he gull me, trow? or is gull'd? Your name, sir?
SIR P.	My name is Politic Would-be.
PER.	[*Aside.*] O, that speaks him.
	A knight, sir?
SIR P.	A poor knight, sir.
PER.	Your lady
	Lies[4] here in Venice, for intelligence
	Of tires and fashions, and behaviour,
	Among the courtesans? The fine Lady Would-be?
SIR P.	Yes, sir; the spider and the bee ofttimes
	Suck from one flower.
PER.	Good Sir Politic,
	I cry you mercy; I have heard much of you:
	'T is true, sir, of your raven.
SIR P.	On your knowledge?
PER.	Yes, and your lion's whelping in the Tower.
SIR P.	Another whelp![5]
PER.	Another, sir.
SIR P.	Now heaven!
	What prodigies be these? The fires at Berwick!
	And the new star! These things concurring, strange,
	And full of omen! Saw you those meteors?
PER.	I did, sir.
SIR P.	Fearful! Pray you, sir, confirm me,
	Were there three porpoises seen above the bridge,
	As they give out?
PER.	Six, and a sturgeon, sir.
SIR P.	I am astonish'd.

---

4. *Lies*] stays.
5. *Another whelp!*] A lion is recorded to have been born in the Tower of London, Aug. 5, 1604, the first born in captivity in England.

PER.	Nay, sir, be not so;
	I'll tell you a greater prodigy than these.
SIR P.	What should these things portend?
PER.	The very day
	(Let me be sure) that I put forth from London,
	There was a whale discover'd in the river,
	As high as Woolwich, that had waited there,
	Few know how many months, for the subversion
	Of the Stode fleet.
SIR P.	Is 't possible? Believe it,
	'T was either sent from Spain, or the archduke's
	Spinola's whale,[6] upon my life, my credit!
	Will they not leave these projects? Worthy sir,
	Some other news.
PER.	Faith, Stone the fool is dead,
	And they do lack a tavern fool extremely.
SIR P.	Is Mass Stone dead?
PER.	He's dead, sir; why, I hope
	You thought him not immortal? — [Aside.] O, this knight,
	Were he well known, would be a precious thing
	To fit our English stage: he that should write
	But such a fellow, should be thought to feign
	Extremely, if not maliciously.
SIR P.	Stone dead!
PER.	Dead. — Lord! how deeply, sir, you apprehend it!
	He was no kinsman to you?
SIR P.	That I know of.
	Well! that same fellow was an unknown fool.
PER.	And yet you knew him, it seems?
SIR P.	I did so. Sir,
	I knew him one of the most dangerous heads
	Living within the state, and so I held him.
PER.	Indeed, sir?
SIR P.	While he liv'd, in action,
	He has receiv'd weekly intelligence,

---

6. 'Twas either sent ... Spinola's whale] Sir Politic believes the whale's presence in the Thames River is some Spanish plot, perhaps directed by Archduke Albert, who ruled the Spanish Netherlands in the name of Philip II, or General Ambrosio Spinola, leader of the Spanish armies in Holland.

> Upon my knowledge, out of the Low Countries,
> For all parts of the world, in cabbages;
> And those dispens'd again to ambassadors,
> In oranges, musk-melons, apricots,
> Lemons, pome-citrons, and such-like; sometimes
> In Colchester oysters, and your Selsey cockles.

PER.   You make me wonder.

SIR P.   Sir, upon my knowledge.
> Nay, I've observ'd him, at your public ordinary,
> Take his advertisement[7] from a traveller,
> A conceal'd statesman, in a trencher of meat;
> And instantly, before the meal was done,
> Convey an answer in a tooth-pick.

PER.   Strange!
> How could this be, sir?

SIR P.   Why, the meat was cut
> So like his character, and so laid as he
> Must easily read the cipher.

PER.   I have heard,
> He could not read, sir.

SIR P.   So 't was given out,
> In policy, by those that did employ him:
> But he could read, and had your languages,
> And to 't, as sound a noddle —

PER.   I have heard, sir,
> That your baboons were spies, and that they were
> A kind of subtle nation near to China.

SIR P.   Ay, ay, your Mamaluchi.[8] Faith, they had
> Their hand in a French plot or two; but they
> Were so extremely giv'n to women, as
> They made discovery of all: yet I
> Had my advices here, on Wednesday last,
> From one of their own coat, they were return'd,
> Made their relations, as the fashion is,
> And now stand fair for fresh employment.

---

7. *advertisement*] information.

8. *Mamaluchi*] Italian form of mamelukes, slaves and warriors originally from Asia Minor, who for many years controlled the throne of Egypt.

PER.   [*Aside.*]   Heart!
        This Sir Pol will be ignorant of nothing. —
        It seems, sir, you know all.

SIR P.   Not all, sir; but
        I have some general notions. I do love
        To note and to observe: though I live out,
        Free from the active torrent, yet I'd mark
        The currents and the passages of things
        For mine own private use; and know the ebbs
        And flows of state.

PER.   Believe it, sir, I hold
        Myself in no small tie[9] unto my fortunes,
        For casting me thus luckily upon you,
        Whose knowledge, if your bounty equal it,
        May do me great assistance, in instruction
        For my behaviour, and my bearing, which
        Is yet so rude and raw.

SIR P.   Why? came you forth
        Empty of rules for travel?

PER.   Faith, I had
        Some common ones, from out that vulgar grammar,
        Which he that cri'd Italian to me, taught me.

SIR P.   Why, this it is that spoils all our brave bloods,
        Trusting our hopeful gentry unto pedants,
        Fellows of outside, and mere bark. You seem
        To be a gentleman of ingenuous race: —
        I not profess it, but my fate hath been
        To be, where I have been consulted with,
        In this high kind, touching some great men's sons,
        Persons of blood and honour. —

PER.   Who be these, sir?

---

9. *tie*] obligation.

SCENE II.

To them enter MOSCA *and* NANO *disguised, followed by persons with materials for erecting a stage.*

MOS.   Under that window, there 't must be. The same.

SIR P.   Fellows, to mount a bank. Did your instructor
        In the dear tongues, never discourse to you
        Of the Italian mountebanks?[1]

PER.   Yes, sir.

SIR P.   Why,
        Here shall you see one.

PER.   They are quacksalvers,
        Fellows that live by venting oils and drugs.

SIR P.   Was that the character he gave you of them?

PER.   As I remember.

SIR P.   Pity his ignorance.
        They are the only knowing men of Europe!
        Great general scholars, excellent physicians,
        Most admir'd statesmen, profest favourites
        And cabinet counsellors to the greatest princes;
        The only languag'd men of all the world!

PER.   And, I have heard, they are most lewd[2] impostors;
        Made all of terms and shreds; no less beliers
        Of great men's favours, than their own vile medicines;
        Which they will utter upon monstrous oaths;
        Selling that drug for twopence, ere they part,
        Which they have valu'd at twelve crowns before.

SIR P.   Sir, calumnies are answer'd best with silence.
        Yourself shall judge. —Who is it mounts, my friends?

MOS.   Scoto of Mantua,[3] sir.

---

1. *mountebanks*] from the Italian *monta in banco,* "to mount the bench," they were part street performer and part patent-medicine salesman.
2. *lewd*] ignorant.
3. *Scoto of Mantua*] a real performer, juggler and magician who visited England and performed before Queen Elizabeth.

SIR P.   Is 't he? Nay, then
I'll proudly promise, sir, you shall behold.
Another man than has been phant'sied[4] to you.
I wonder yet, that he should mount his bank,
Here in this nook, that has been wont t' appear
In face of the Piazza! — Here he comes.

[*Enter* VOLPONE, *disguised as a mountebank Doctor, and followed by a crowd of people.*]

VOLP.   Mount, zany. [*To* NANO.]
MOB.   Follow, follow, follow, follow!
SIR P.   See how the people follow him! he's a man
May write ten thousand crowns in bank here. Note,
                       [VOLPONE *mounts the stage.*]
Mark but his gesture: — I do use to observe
The state he keeps in getting up.
PER.   'T is worth it, sir.
VOLP.   "Most noble gentlemen, and my worthy patrons! It may seem
strange that I, your Scoto Mantuano, who was ever wont to
fix my bank in the face of the public Piazza, near the shelter
of the Portico to the Procuratia, should now, after eight
months' absence from this illustrious city of Venice, humbly retire myself into an obscure nook of the Piazza."
SIR P.   Did not I now object the same?
PER.   Peace, sir.
VOLP.   "Let me tell you: I am not, as your Lombard proverb saith,
cold on my feet; or content to part with my commodities at
a cheaper rate than I am accustom'd: look not for it. Nor
that the calumnious reports of that impudent detractor, and
shame to our profession (Alessandro Buttone, I mean), who
gave out, in public, I was condemn'd *a' sforzato*[5] to the
galleys, for poisoning the Cardinal Bembo's — cook, hath at
all attach'd, much less dejected me. No, no, worthy gentlemen; to tell you true, I cannot endure to see the rabble of
these ground *ciarlitani*,[6] that spread their cloaks on the
pavement, as if they meant to do feats of activity, and then

4. *phant'sied*] described, misrepresented.
5. a' sforzato] to hard labor.
6. ciarlitani] petty charlatans, imposters.

come in lamely, with their mouldy tales out of Boccacio, like stale Tabarin,[7] the fabulist: some of them discoursing their travels, and of their tedious captivity in the Turk's galleys, when, indeed, were the truth known, they were the Christian's galleys, where very temperately they eat bread, and drunk water, as a wholesome penance, enjoin'd them by their confessors, for base pilferies."

SIR P.   Note but his bearing, and contempt of these.

VOLP.   "These turdy-facy-nasty-paty-lousy-fartical rogues, with one poor groat's-worth of unprepar'd antimony, finely wrapt up in several *scartoccios*,[8] are able, very well, to kill their twenty a week, and play; yet these meagre, starv'd spirits, who have half stopt the organs of their minds with earthy oppilations,[9] want not their favourers among your shrivell'd salad-eating artisans, who are overjoy'd that they may have their half-pe'rth of physic; though it purge 'em into another world, 't makes no matter."

SIR P.   Excellent! ha' you heard better language, sir?

VOLP.   "Well, let 'em go. And, gentlemen, honourable gentlemen, know, that for this time, our bank, being thus removed from the clamours of the *canaglia*[10] shall be the scene of pleasure and delight; for I have nothing to sell, little or nothing to sell."

SIR P.   I told you, sir, his end.

PER.   You did so, sir.

VOLP.   "I protest, I, and my six servants, are not able to make of this precious liquor so fast as it is fetch'd away from my lodging by gentlemen of your city; strangers of the Terra-firma;[11] worshipful merchants; ay, and senators too: who, ever since my arrival, have detain'd me to their uses, by their splendidous liberalities. And worthily; for, what avails your rich man to have his magazines stuft with *moscadelli*, or of the purest grape, when his physicians prescribe him, on pain of

---

7. *Tabarin*] a French charlatan of the early seventeenth century, whose jests were published.
8. scartoccios] folds of paper.
9. *oppilations*] obstructions.
10. canaglia] rabble.
11. *Terra-firma*] Continental possessions of Venice.

death, to drink nothing but water cocted[12] with aniseeds? O
health! health! the blessing of the rich! the riches of the
poor! who can buy thee at too dear a rate, since there is no
enjoying this world without thee? Be not then so sparing of
your purses, honourable gentlemen, as to abridge the natu-
ral course of life—"

PER. You see his end.

SIR P.   Ay, is 't not good?

VOLP. "For when a humid flux, or catarrh, by the mutability of air,
falls from your head into an arm or shoulder, or any other
part; take you a ducket, or your chequin of gold, and apply
to the place affected: see what good effect it can work. No,
no, 't is this blessed *unguento*,[13] this rare extraction, that
hath only power to disperse all malignant humours, that
proceed either of hot, cold, moist, or windy causes—"

PER. I would he had put in dry too.

SIR P.   Pray you observe.

VOLP. "To fortify the most indigest and crude stomach, ay, were it of
one that, through extreme weakness, vomited blood, applying only a warm napkin to the place, after the unction and
fricace;[14]—for the *vertigine*[15] in the head, putting but a
drop into your nostrils, likewise behind the ears; a most
sovereign and approv'd remedy; the *mal caduco*,[16] cramps,
convulsions, paralyses, epilepsies, *tremorcordia*, retir'd
nerves, ill vapours of the spleen, stoppings of the liver, the
stone, the strangury, *hernia ventosa, iliaca passio*;[17] stops a
dysenteria immediately; easeth the torsion[18] of the small
guts; and cures *melancholia hypocondriaca*, being taken
and appli'd, according to my printed receipt. (*Pointing to
his bill and his glass.*) For this is the physician, this the
medicine; this counsels, this cures; this gives the direction,
this works the effect; and, in sum, both together may be

12. *cocted*] boiled.
13. unguento] ointment.
14. *fricace*] an oil to be rubbed in.
15. vertigine] dizziness.
16. mal caduco] epilepsy.
17. hernia ventosa, iliaca passio] gassy hernia, cramps of the small intestine.
18. *torsion*] twisting.

term'd an abstract of the theoric and practic in the Aescula-
pian art. 'T will cost you eight crowns. And, —Zan Fritada,
prithee sing a verse extempore in honour of it."

SIR P.　How do you like him, sir?
PER.　　　　　　　　Most strangely, I!
SIR P.　Is not his language rare?
PER.　　　　　　　　But alchemy,
I never heard the like; or Broughton's[19] books.

[NANO *sings.*]

> Had old Hippocrates, or Galen,
> That to their books put med'cines all in,
> But known this secret, they had never
> (Of which they will be guilty ever)
> Been murderers of so much paper,
> Or wasted many a hurtless taper;
> No Indian drug had e'er been fam'd,
> Tobacco, sassafras not nam'd;
> Ne yet of guacum one small stick, sir,
> Nor Raymund Lully's[20] great elixir.
> Ne had been known the Danish Gonswart,[21]
> Or Paracelsus, with his long sword.[22]

PER.　All this, yet, will not do; eight crowns is high.
VOLP.　"No more. — Gentlemen, if I had but time to discourse to you
the miraculous effects of this my oil, surnam'd Oglio del
Scoto; with the countless catalogue of those I have cur'd of
th' aforesaid, and many more diseases; the patents and
privileges of all the princes and commonwealths of Chris-
tendom; or but the depositions of those that appear'd on my
part, before the signiory of the Sanita and most learned
College of Physicians; where I was authoris'd, upon notice
taken of the admirable virtues of my medicaments, and
mine own excellency in matter of rare and unknown secrets, not only to disperse them publicly in this famous city,
but in all the territories, that happily joy under the govern-

19. *Broughton's books*] Hugh Broughton, a Puritan divine and rabbinical scholar.
20. *Raymond Lully*] a Spanish mystic philosopher (ca. 1235–1316).
21. *Gonswart*] unidentified.
22. *Paracelsus*] famous 16th-century German doctor, who carried his familiar spirits in the
handle of his sword.

ment of the most pious and magnificent states of Italy. But may some other gallant fellow say, 'O, there be divers that make profession to have as good, and as experimented receipts as yours:' indeed, very many have assay'd, like apes, in imitation of that, which is really and essentially in me, to make of this oil; bestow'd great cost in furnaces, stills, alembics,[23] continual fires, and preparation of the ingredients (as indeed there goes to it six hundred several simples, besides some quantity of human fat, for the conglutination, which we buy of the anatomists), but when these practitioners come to the last decoction, blow, blow, puff, puff, and all flies in fumo:[24] ha, ha, ha! Poor wretches! I rather pity their folly and indiscretion, than their loss of time and money; for those may be recover'd by industry: but to be a fool born, is a disease incurable.

"For myself, I always from my youth have endeavour'd to get the rarest secrets, and book them, either in exchange, or for money; I spar'd nor cost nor labour, where anything was worthy to be learned. And, gentlemen, honourable gentlemen, I will undertake, by virtue of chymical art, out of the honourable hat that covers your head, to extract the four elements; that is to say, the fire, air, water, and earth, and return you your felt without burn or stain. For, whilst others have been at the *ballo*,[25] I have been at my book; and am now past the craggy paths of study, and come to the flowery plains of honour and reputation."

SIR P.   I do assure you, sir, that is his aim.
VOLP.   "But to our price—"
PER.   And that withal, Sir Pol.
VOLP.   "You all know, honourable gentlemen, I never valu'd this *ampulla*, or vial, at less than eight crowns; but for this time, I am content to be depriv'd of it for six; six crowns is the price, and less in courtesy I know you cannot offer me; take it or leave it, howsoever, both it and I am at your service. I ask you not as the value of the thing, for then I should demand of you a thousand crowns, so the Cardinals Mon-

23. *alembics*] distilleries, also retorts.
24. *in fumo*] in smoke.
25. ballo] ball; dancing.

talto, Fernese, the great Duke of Tuscany, my gossip,[26] with
divers other princes, have given me; but I despise money.
Only to show my affection to you, honourable gentlemen,
and your illustrious State here, I have neglected the mes-
sages of these princes, mine own offices, fram'd my journey
hither, only to present you with the fruits of my travels. —
Tune your voices once more to the touch of your instru-
ments, and give the honourable assembly some delightful
recreation."

PER. What monstrous and most painful circumstance
Is here, to get some three or four gazettes,[27]
Some threepence i' the whole! for that 't will come to.

[NANO *sings*.]

You that would last long, list to my song,
Make no more coil, but buy of this oil.
Would you be ever fair and young?
Stout of teeth, and strong of tongue?
Tart of palate? quick of ear?
Sharp of sight? of nostril clear?
Moist of hand? and light of foot?
Or, I will come nearer to 't,
Would you live free from all diseases?
Do the act your mistress pleases,
Yet fright all aches from your bones?
Here's a med'cine for the nones.[28]

VOLP. "Well, I am in a humour at this time to make a present of the
small quantity my coffer contains; to the rich in courtesy,
and to the poor for God's sake. Wherefore now mark: I ask'd
you six crowns; and six crowns, at other times, you have
paid me; you shall not give me six crowns, nor five, nor four,
nor three, nor two, nor one; nor half a ducat; no, nor a
moccinigo.[29] Sixpence it will cost you, or six hundred
pound — expect no lower price, for, by the banner of my
front, I will not bate a bagatine,[30] — that I will have, only, a
pledge of your loves, to carry something from amongst you,

26. *gossip*] literally god-parent; usually, familiar friend.
27. *gazettes*] small Venetian coins.
28. *for the nones*] for the purpose.
29. moccinigo] a coin used in Venice, worth about ninepence.
30. *bagatine*] an Italian coin worth about one-third of a farthing.

to show I am not contemn'd by you. Therefore, now, toss your handkerchiefs, cheerfully, cheerfully; and be advertis'd, that the first heroic spirit that deigns to grace me with a handkerchief, I will give it a little remembrance of something beside, shall please it better than if I had presented it with a double pistolet."[31]

PER.   Will you be that heroic spark, Sir Pol?

       CELIA, *at the window, throws down her handkerchief.*
       O, see! the windore has prevented[32] you.

VOLP.   "Lady, I kiss your bounty; and for this timely grace you have done your poor Scoto of Mantua, I will return you, over and above my oil, a secret of that high and inestimable nature, shall make you for ever enamour'd on that minute, wherein your eye first descended on so mean, yet not altogether to be despis'd, an object. Here is a powder conceal'd in this paper, of which, if I should speak to the worth, nine thousand volumes were but as one page, that page as a line, that line as a word; so short is this pilgrimage of man (which some call life) to the expressing of it. Would I reflect on the price? Why, the whole world is but as an empire, that empire as a province, that province as a bank, that bank as a private purse to the purchase of it. I will only tell you; it is the powder that made Venus a goddess (given her by Apollo), that kept her perpetually young, clear'd her wrinkles, firm'd her gums, fill'd her skin, colour'd her hair; from her deriv'd to Helen, and at the sack of Troy unfortunately lost: till now, in this our age, it was as happily recover'd, by a studious antiquary, out of some ruins of Asia, who sent a moiety of it to the court of France (but much sophisticated), wherewith the ladies there now colour their hair. The rest, at this present, remains with me; extracted to a quintessence: so that, wherever it but touches, in youth it perpetually preserves, in age restores the complexion; seats your teeth, did they dance like virginal jacks,[33] firm as a wall: makes them white as ivory, that were black as — "

31. *pistolet*] a Spanish coin.
32. *prevented*] anticipated.
33. *virginal jacks*] small pieces of wood to which were attached the quills which struck the strings of the virginal.

SCENE III. — *The same*

To them enter CORVINO.

COR. Spite o' the devil, and my shame! come down here;
Come down! — No house but mine to make your scene?
Signior Flaminio, will you down, sir? down?
What, is my wife your Franciscina, sir?
No windows on the whole Piazza, here,
To make your properties, but mine? but mine?
                    Beats away [VOLPONE, NANO, *etc.*]
Heart! ere to-morrow I shall be new christen'd,
And called the Pantalone di Besogniosi,[1]
About the town.

PER.   What should this mean, Sir Pol?
SIR P. Some trick of state, believe it; I will home.
PER. It may be some design on you.
SIR P.   I know not.
I'll stand upon my guard.
PER.   It is your best, sir.
SIR P. This three weeks, all my advices, all my letters.
They have been intercepted.
PER.   Indeed, sir!
Best have a care.
SIR P.   Nay, so I will.
PER. This knight,
I may not lose him, for my mirth, till night.

                              [*Exeunt.*]

---

1. *Pantalone di Besogniosi*] Italian for "Fool of the Beggars."

SCENE IV. — *A room in Volpone's house*

Enter VOLPONE, MOSCA.

VOLP.   O, I am wounded!

MOS.   Where, sir?

VOLP.   Not without;
Those blows were nothing: I could bear them ever.
But angry Cupid, bolting from her eyes,
Hath shot himself into me like a flame;
Where now he flings about his burning heat,
As in a furnace an ambitious fire
Whose vent is stopt. The fight is all within me.
I cannot live, except thou help me, Mosca;
My liver melts, and I, without the hope
Of some soft air from her refreshing breath,
Am but a heap of cinders.

MOS.   'Las, good sir,
Would you had never seen her!

VOLP.   Nay, would thou
Hadst never told me of her!

MOS.   Sir, 't is true;
I do confess I was unfortunate,
And you unhappy; but I 'm bound in conscience,
No less than duty, to effect my best
To your release of torment, and I will, sir.

VOLP.   Dear Mosca, shall I hope?

MOS.   Sir, more than dear,
I will not bid you to despair of aught
Within a human compass.

VOLP.   O, there spoke
My better angel. Mosca, take my keys,
Gold, plate, and jewels, all 's at thy devotion;[1]
Employ them how thou wilt: nay, coin me too:
So thou in this but crown my longings, Mosca.

---

1. *at thy devotion*] at your service.

Mos.	Use but your patience.
Volp.	So I have.
Mos.	I doubt not.
	To bring success to your desires.
Volp.	Nay, then,
	I not repent me of my late disguise.
Mos.	If you can horn him, sir, you need not.
Volp.	True:
	Besides, I never meant him for my heir.
	Is not the colour o' my beard and eyebrows
	To make me known?
Mos.	No jot.
Volp.	I did it well.
Mos.	So well, would I could follow you in mine,
	With half the happiness! and yet I would
	Escape your epilogue.[2]
Volp.	But were they gull'd
	With a belief that I was Scoto?
Mos.	Sir,
	Scoto himself could hardly have distinguish'd!
	I have not time to flatter you now; we'll part:
	And as I prosper, so applaud my art. [*Exeunt.*]

SCENE V. — *A room in Corvino's house*

Enter CORVINO, *with his sword in his hand, dragging in* CELIA.

Corv.	Death of mine honour, with the city's fool!
	A juggling, tooth-drawing, prating mountebank!
	And at a public windore! where, whilst he,
	With his strain'd action, and his dole of faces,[1]
	To his drug-lecture draws your itching ears,
	A crew of old, unmarri'd, noted lechers,

2. *your epilogue*] i.e., the beating from Corvino.

---

1. *faces*] grimaces.

Stood leering up like satyrs: and you smile
Most graciously, and fan your favours forth,
To give your hot spectators satisfaction!
What, was your mountbank their call? their whistle?
Or were you enamour'd on his copper rings,
His saffron jewel, with the toad-stone in 't,
Or his embroid'red suit, with the cope-stitch,
Made of a hearse cloth? or his old tilt-feather?
Or his starch'd beard! Well, you shall have him, yes!
He shall come home, and minister unto you
The fricace for the mother.[2] Or, let me see,
I think you'd rather mount; would you not mount?
Why, if you'll mount, you may; yes, truly, you may!
And so you may be seen, down to the foot.
Get you a cittern,[3] Lady Vanity,
And be a dealer with the virtuous man;
Make one. I'll but protest myself a cuckold,
And save your dowry. I'm a Dutchman, I!
For if you thought me an Italian,
You would be damn'd ere you did this, you whore!
Thou 'dst tremble to imagine that the murder
Of father, mother, brother, all thy race,
Should follow, as the subject of my justice.

CEL.   Good sir, have patience.

CORV.   What couldst thou propose[4]
Less to thyself, than in this heat of wrath,
And stung with my dishonour, I should strike
This steel into thee, with as many stabs
As thou wert gaz'd upon with goatish eyes?

CEL.   Alas, sir, be appeas'd! I could not think
My being at the windore should more now
Move your impatience than at other times.

CORV.   No! not to seek and entertain a parley
With a known knave, before a multitude!
You were an actor with your handkerchief,
Which he most sweetly kist in the receipt,

---

2. *fricace for the mother*] massage for the womb.
3. *cittern*] a kind of guitar.
4. *propose*] expect.

	And might, no doubt, return it with a letter,

And might, no doubt, return it with a letter,
And point the place where you might meet; your sister's,
Your mother's, or your aunt's might serve the turn.

CEL. Why, dear sir, when do I make these excuses,
Or ever stir abroad, but to the church?
And that so seldom —

CORV. Well, it shall be less;
And thy restraint before was liberty,
To what I now decree: and therefore mark me.
First, I will have this bawdy light damm'd up;[5]
And till 't be done, some two or three yards off,
I'll chalk a line; o'er which if thou but chance
To set thy desp'rate foot, more hell, more horror,
More wild remorseless rage shall seize on thee,
Than on a conjuror that had heedless left
His circle's safety ere his devil was laid.
Then here's a lock which I will hang upon thee,
And, now I think on 't, I will keep thee backwards;
Thy lodging shall be backwards: thy walks backwards;
Thy prospect, all be backwards; and no pleasure,
That thou shalt know but backwards: nay, since you force
My honest nature, know, it is your own,
Being too open, makes me use you thus:
Since you will not contain your subtle nostrils
In a sweet room, but they must snuff the air
Of rank and sweaty passengers. (*Knock within.*) One knocks.
Away, and be not seen, pain of thy life;
Nor look toward the windore; if thou dost —
Nay, stay, hear this — let me not prosper, whore,
But I will make thee an anatomy,
Dissect thee mine own self, and read a lecture
Upon thee to the city, and in public.
Away! — [*Exit* CELIA.]

[*Enter* SERVANT.]

Who's there?

SER. 'T is Signior Mosca, sir.

---

5. *bawdy light dammed up*] i.e., brick up the window.

SCENE VI. — *The same*

CORVINO. *Enter* MOSCA.

CORV.   Let him come in. His master's dead; there's yet
        Some good to help the bad. — My Mosca, welcome!
        I guess your news.

MOS.   I fear you cannot, sir.

CORV.   Is 't not his death?

MOS.   Rather the contrary.

CORV.   Not his recovery?

MOS.   Yes, sir.

CORV.   I am curs'd,
        I am bewitch'd, my crosses meet to vex me.
        How? how? how? how?

MOS.   Why, sir, with Scoto's oil;
        Corbaccio and Voltore brought of it,
        Whilst I was busy in an inner room —

CORV.   Death! that damn'd mountebank! but for the law
        Now, I could kill the rascal: it cannot be
        His oil should have that virtue. Ha' not I
        Known him a common rogue, come fiddling in
        To the *osteria*,[1] with a tumbling whore,
        And, when he has done all his forc'd tricks, been glad
        Of a poor spoonful of dead wine, with flies in 't?
        It cannot be. All his ingredients
        Are a sheep's gall, a roasted bitch's marrow,
        Some few sod[2] earwigs, pounded caterpillars,
        A little capon's grease, and fasting spittle:[3]
        I know them to a dram.

MOS.   I know not, sir;
        But some on 't, there, they pour'd into his ears,

---

1. *osteria*] inn.
2. *sod*] boiled.
3. *fasting spittle*] spit from a hungry man.

	Some in his nostrils, and recover'd him;
	Applying but the fricace.[4]
CORV.	Pox o' that fricace!
MOS.	And since, to seem the more officious
	And flatt'ring of his health, there, they have had,
	At extreme fees, the college of physicians
	Consulting on him, how they might restore him;
	Where one would have a cataplasm[5] of spices,
	Another a flay'd ape clapp'd to his breast,
	A third would have it a dog, a fourth an oil,
	With wild cats' skins: at last, they all resolv'd
	That to preserve him, was no other means
	But some young woman must be straight sought out,
	Lusty, and full of juice, to sleep by him;
	And to this service most unhappily,
	And most unwillingly, am I now employ'd,
	Which here I thought to pre-acquaint you with,
	For your advice, since it concerns you most;
	Because I would not do that thing might cross
	Your ends, on whom I have my whole dependence, sir;
	Yet, if I do it not they may delate[6]
	My slackness to my patron, work me out
	Of his opinion; and there all your hopes,
	Ventures, or whatsoever, are all frustrate!
	I do but tell you, sir. Besides, they are all
	Now striving who shall first present him; therefore —
	I could entreat you, briefly conclude somewhat;
	Prevent 'em if you can.
CORV.	Death to my hopes,
	This is my villanous fortune! Best to hire
	Some common courtesan.
MOS.	Ay, I thought on that, sir;
	But they are all so subtle, full of art —
	And age again doting and flexible,
	So as — I cannot tell — we may, perchance,
	Light on a quean may cheat us all.

---

4. *Applying but the fricace*] All they had to do was rub it in.
5. *cataplasm*] poultice.
6. *delate*] denounce, complain of.

CORV.	'T is true.
MOS.	No, no: it must be one that has no tricks, sir,
	Some simple thing, a creature made[7] unto it;
	Some wench you may command. Ha' you no kinswoman?
	Gods so — Think, think, think, think, think, think, think, sir.
	One o' the doctors offer'd there his daughter.
CORV.	How!
MOS.	Yes, Signior Lupo, the physician.
CORV.	His daughter!
MOS.	And a virgin, sir. Why, alas,
	He knows the state of 's body, what it is:
	That nought can warm his blood, sir, but a fever;
	Nor any incantation raise his spirit:
	A long forgetfulness hath seiz'd that part.
	Besides, sir, who shall know it? Some one or two —
CORV.	I pray thee give me leave. [*Walks aside.*] If any man
	But I had had this luck — The thing in 't self,
	I know, is nothing. — Wherefore should not I
	As well command my blood and my affections
	As this dull doctor? In the point of honour,
	The cases are all one of wife and daughter.
MOS.	[*Aside.*] I hear him coming.[8]
CORV.	She shall do 't: 't is done.
	Slight! if this doctor, who is not engag'd,
	Unless 't be for his counsel, which is nothing,
	Offer his daughter, what should I, that am
	So deeply in? I will prevent him: Wretch!
	Covetous wretch! — Mosca, I have determin'd.
MOS.	How, sir?
CORV.	We'll make all sure. The party you wot of
	Shall be mine own wife, Mosca.
MOS.	Sir, the thing,
	But that I would not seem to counsel you,
	I should have motion'd to you, at the first:
	And make your count, you have cut all their throats.
	Why, 't is directly taking a possession!
	And in his next fit, we may let him go.

7. *made unto it*] prepared for it.
8. *coming*] into the trap.

'T is but to pull the pillow from his head,
And he is throttled: it had been done before
But for your scrupulous doubts.

CORV.   Ay, a plague on 't,
My conscience fools my wit! Well, I'll be brief,
And so be thou, lest they should be before us.
Go home, prepare him, tell him with what zeal
And willingness I do it: swear it was
On the first hearing, as thou mayst do, truly,
Mine own free motion.

MOS.   Sir, I warrant you,
I'll so possess him with it, that the rest
Of his starv'd clients shall be banish'd all;
And only you receiv'd. But come not, sir,
Until I send, for I have something else
To ripen for your good, you must not know 't.

CORV.   But do not you forget to send now.

MOS.   Fear not. [*Exit.*]

SCENE VII. — *The same*

CORVINO.

CORV.   Where are you, wife? My Celia! wife!

[*Enter* CELIA.]

                              —What, blubb'ring?
Come, dry those tears. I think thou thought'st me in earnest;
Ha! by this light I talk'd so but to try thee:
Methinks, the lightness of the occasion
Should have confirm'd thee. Come, I am not jealous.

CEL.   No?

CORV.   Faith I am not, I, nor never was;
It is a poor unprofitable humour.
Do not I know, if women have a will,
They'll do 'gainst all the watches o' the world,
And that the fiercest spies are tam'd with gold?

Tut, I am confident in thee, thou shalt see 't;
And see I'll give thee cause too, to believe it.
Come kiss me. Go, and make thee ready straight,
In all thy best attire, thy choicest jewels,
Put 'em all on, and, with 'em, thy best looks:
We are invited to a solemn feast,
At old Volpone's, where it shall appear
How far I am free from jealousy or fear.

                                        [*Exeunt.*]

ACT III

SCENE I. — A street

Enter MOSCA.

MOS. I fear I shall begin to grow in love
   With my dear self, and my most prosp'rous parts,
   They do so spring and burgeon; I can feel
   A whimsy in my blood: I know not how,
   Success hath made me wanton. I could skip
   Out of my skin now, like a subtle snake,
   I am so limber. O! your parasite
   Is a most precious thing, dropt from above,
   Not bred 'mongst clods and clodpoles, here on earth.
   I muse, the mystery[1] was not made a science,
   It is so liberally profest! Almost
   All the wise world is little else, in nature,
   But parasites or sub-parasites. And yet
   I mean not those that have your bare town-art,
   To know who's fit to feed them; have no house,
   No family, no care, and therefore mould
   Tales for men's ears, to bait that sense; or get
   Kitchen-invention, and some stale receipts
   To please the belly, and the groin; nor those,
   With their court dog-tricks, that can fawn and fleer,
   Make their revenue out of legs[2] and faces,
   Echo my lord, and lick away a moth:
   But your fine elegant rascal, that can rise

1. *mystery*] craft, profession.
2. *legs*] bows.

And stoop, almost together, like an arrow;
Shoot through the air as nimbly as a star;
Turn short as doth a swallow; and be here,
And there, and here, and yonder, all at once;
Present to any humour, all occasion;
And change a visor swifter than a thought!
This is the creature had the art born with him;
Toils not to learn it, but doth practise it
Out of most excellent nature: and such sparks
Are the true parasites, others but their zanies.

SCENE II. — *The same*

MOSCA. *Enter* BONARIO.

    Who's this? Bonario, old Corbaccio's son?
    The person I was bound to seek. Fair sir,
    You are happ'ly met.

BON.   That cannot be by thee.

MOS.   Why, sir?

BON.   Nay, pray thee know thy way, and leave me:
    I would be loth to interchange discourse
    With such a mate[1] as thou art.

MOS.   Courteous sir,
    Scorn not my poverty.

BON.   Not I, by heaven;
    But thou shalt give me leave to hate thy baseness.

MOS.   Baseness!

BON.   Ay; answer me, is not thy sloth
    Sufficient argument? thy flattery?
    Thy means of feeding?

MOS.   Heaven be good to me!
    These imputations are too common, sir,
    And easily stuck on virtue when she's poor.
    You are unequal[2] to me, and however

---

1. *mate*] fellow.
2. *unequal*] unfair.

Your sentence may be righteous, yet you are not,
That, ere you know me, thus proceed in censure:
St. Mark bear witness 'gainst you, 't is inhuman.

                                                  [*Weeps.*]

BON.   [*Aside.*] What! does he weep? the sign is soft and good:
          I do repent me that I was so harsh.

MOS.   'T is true, that, sway'd by strong necessity,
          I am enforc'd to eat my careful bread
          With too much obsequy; 't is true, beside,
          That I am fain to spin mine own poor raiment
          Out of my mere observance, being not born
          To a free fortune: but that I have done
          Base offices, in rending friends asunder,
          Dividing families, betraying counsels,
          Whisp'ring false lies, or mining men with praises,
          Train'd their credulity with perjuries,
          Corrupted chastity, or am in love
          With mine own tender ease, but would not rather
          Prove the most rugged and laborious course,
          That might redeem my present estimation,
          Let me here perish, in all hope of goodness.

BON.   [*Aside.*] This cannot be a personated passion. —
          I was to blame, so to mistake thy nature;
          Prithee forgive me: and speak out thy business.

MOS.   Sir, it concerns you; and though I may seem
          At first to make a main offence in manners,
          And in my gratitude unto my master,
          Yet for the pure love which I bear all right,
          And hatred of the wrong, I must reveal it.
          This very hour your father is in purpose
          To disinherit you —

BON.   How!
MOS.   And thrust you forth,
          As a mere stranger to his blood: 't is true, sir.
          The work no way engageth me, but as
          I claim an interest in the general state
          Of goodness and true virtue, which I hear
          T' abound in you; and for which mere respect,
          Without a second aim, sir, I have done it.

BON.   This tale hath lost thee much of the late trust

MOS. It is a confidence that well becomes
     Your piety; and form'd, no doubt, it is
     From your own simple innocence: which makes
     Your wrong more monstrous and abhorr'd. But, sir,
     I now will tell you more. This very minute,
     It is, or will be doing; and if you
     Shall be but pleas'd to go with me, I'll bring you,
     I dare not say where you shall see, but where
     Your ear shall be a witness of the deed;
     Hear yourself written bastard, and profest
     The common issue of the earth.

BON.   I 'm maz'd!

MOS. Sir, if I do it not, draw your just sword,
     And score your vengeance on my front and face;
     Mark me your villain: you have too much wrong,
     And I do suffer for you, sir. My heart
     Weeps blood in anguish —

BON.   Lead; I follow thee.   [*Exeunt.*]

SCENE III. — *A room in Volpone's house*

Enter VOLPONE, NANO, ANDROGYNO, CASTRONE.

VOLP. Mosca stays long, methinks. — Bring forth your sports,
     And help to make the wretched time more sweet.

NAN. "Dwarf, fool, and eunuch, well met here we be.
     A question it were now, whether of us three,
     Being all the known delicates of a rich man,
     In pleasing him, claim the precedency can?"

CAS. "I claim for myself."

AND.   "And so doth the fool."

NAN. " 'T is foolish indeed: let me set you both to school.
     First for your dwarf, he's little and witty,
     And everything, as it is little, is pretty;

Else why do men say to a creature of my shape,
So soon as they see him, 'It's a pretty little ape'?
And why a pretty ape, but for pleasing imitation
Of greater men's actions, in a ridiculous fashion?
Beside, this feat[1] body of mine doth not crave
Half the meat, drink, and cloth, one of your bulks will have.
Admit your fool's face be the mother of laughter,
Yet, for his brain, it must always come after:
And though that do feed him, it's a pitiful case,
His body is beholding to such a bad face."

One knocks.

VOLP.   Who's there? My couch; away! look! Nano, see: [*Exeunt* AND.
     and CAS.]
     Give me my caps first — go, inquire. [*Exit* NANO.] Now, Cu-
     pid
     Send it be Mosca, and with fair return!
NAN.   [*within.*] It is the beauteous madam —
VOLP.   Would-be — is it?
NAN.   The same.
VOLP.   Now torment on me! Squire her in;
     For she will enter, or dwell here for ever:
     Nay, quickly. [*Retires to his couch.*] That my fit were past!
     I fear
     A second hell too, that my loathing this
     Will quite expel my appetite to the other:
     Would she were taking now her tedious leave.
     Lord, how it threats me what I am to suffer!

1. *feat*] neatly made.

SCENE IV. — *The same*

To him enter NANO, LADY POLITIC WOULD-BE.

LADY P.   I thank you, good sir. Pray you signify
      Unto your patron I am here. — This band
      Shows not my neck enough. — I trouble you, sir;
      Let me request you bid one of my women
      Come hither to me. In good faith, I am drest
      Most favourably to-day! It is no matter:
      'T is well enough.

[*Enter* 1st Waiting-woman.]

                           Look, see these petulant things,
      How they have done this!

VOLP.   [*Aside.*] I do feel the fever
      Ent'ring in at mine ears; O, for a charm,
      To fright it hence!

LADY P.   Come nearer: is this curl
      In his right place, or this? Why is this higher
      Than all the rest? You ha' not wash'd your eyes yet!
      Or do they not stand even i' your head?
      Where is your fellow? call her. [*Exit* 1st Woman.]

NAN.   Now, St. Mark
      Deliver us! anon she'll beat her women,
      Because her nose is red.

[*Re-enter* 1st *with* 2nd Woman.]

LADY P.   I pray you view
      This tire,[1] forsooth: are all things apt, or no?

1ST WOM.   One hair a little here sticks out, forsooth.

LADY P.   Does 't so, forsooth! and where was your dear sight,
      When it did so, forsooth! What now! bird-ey'd?[2]
      And you, too? Pray you, both approach and mend it.
      Now, by that light I muse you're not asham'd!

---

1. *tire*] head-dress.
2. *bird-ey'd*] sharp-sighted.

	I, that have preach'd these things so oft unto you,
	Read you the principles, argu'd all the grounds,
	Disputed every fitness, every grace,
	Call'd you to counsel of so frequent dressings—
NAN.	(*Aside.*) More carefully than of your fame or honour.
LADY P.	Made you acquainted what an ample dowry
	The knowledge of these things would be unto you,
	Able alone to get you noble husbands
	At your return: and you thus to neglect it!
	Besides, you seeing what a curious nation
	Th' Italians are, what will they say of me?
	"The English lady cannot dress herself."
	Here's a fine imputation to our country!
	Well, go your ways, and stay i' the next room.
	This fucus[3] was too coarse too; it's no matter.—
	Good sir, you'll give 'em entertainment?
	[*Exeunt* NANO *and* Waiting-women.]
VOLP.	The storm comes toward me.
LADY P.	[*Goes to the couch.*] How does my Volpone?
VOLP.	Troubl'd with noise, I cannot sleep; I dreamt
	That a strange fury ent'red now my house,
	And, with the dreadful tempest of her breath,
	Did cleave my roof asunder.
LADY P.	Believe me, and I
	Had the most fearful dream, could I remember 't—
VOLP.	[*Aside.*] Out on my fate! I have given her the occasion
	How to torment me: she will tell me hers.
LADY P.	Methought the golden mediocrity,
	Polite, and delicate—
VOLP.	O, if you do love me,
	No more: I sweat, and suffer, at the mention
	Of any dream; feel how I tremble yet.
LADY P.	Alas, good soul! the passion of the heart.
	Seed-pearl were good now, boil'd with syrup of apples,
	Tincture of gold, and coral, citron-pills,
	Your elecampane[4] root, myrobalanes[5]—
VOLP.	Ay me, I have ta'en a grasshopper by the wing!

3. *fucus*] face paint.
4. *elecampane*] horse-heal, a medicinal herb.
5. *myrobalanes*] an astringent kind of plum.

LADY P.	Burnt silk and amber. You have muscadel
	Good i' the house —
VOLP.	You will not drink, and part?
LADY P.	No, fear not that. I doubt we shall not get
	Some English saffron, half a dram would serve;
	Your sixteen cloves, a little musk, dried mints;
	Bugloss, and barley-meal —
VOLP.	[*Aside.*] She's in again!
	Before I feign'd diseases, now I have one.
LADY P.	And these appli'd with a right scarlet cloth.
VOLP.	[*Aside.*] Another flood of words! a very torrent!
LADY P.	Shall I, sir, make you a poultice?
VOLP.	No, no, no.
	I'm very well, you need prescribe no more.
LADY P.	I have a little studied physic; but now
	I'm all for music, save, i' the forenoons,
	An hour or two for painting. I would have
	A lady, indeed, to have all letters and arts,
	Be able to discourse, to write, to paint,
	But principal, as Plato holds, your music,
	And so does wise Pythagoras, I take it,
	Is your true rapture: when there is concent[6]
	In face, in voice, and clothes: and is, indeed,
	Our sex's chiefest ornament.
VOLP.	The poet
	As old in time as Plato, and as knowing,
	Says that your highest female grace is silence.
LADY P.	Which of your poets? Petrarch, or Tasso, or Dante?
	Guarini? Ariosto? Aretine?
	Cieco di Hadria? I have read them all.
VOLP.	[*Aside.*] Is everything a cause to my destruction?
LADY P.	I think I have two or three of 'em about me.
VOLP.	[*Aside.*] The sun, the sea, will sooner both stand still
	Than her eternal tongue! nothing can scape it.
LADY P.	Here's Pastor Fido —
VOLP.	[*Aside.*] Profess obstinate silence;
	That's now my safest.
LADY P.	All our English writers,
	I mean such as are happy in th' Italian,

6. *concent*] harmony.

Will deign to steal out of this author, mainly;
Almost as much as from Montagnié:
He has so modern and facile a vein,
Fitting the time, and catching the court-ear!
Your Petrarch is more passionate, yet he,
In days of sonnetting, trusted 'em with much:
Dante is hard, and few can understand him.
But for a desperate wit, there's Aretine;
Only his pictures are a little obscene —
You mark me not.

VOLP.   Alas, my mind's perturb'd.

LADY P. Why, in such cases, we must cure ourselves,
Make use of our philosophy —

VOLP.   Oh me!

LADY P. And as we find our passions do rebel,
Encounter them with reason, or divert 'em,
By giving scope unto some other humour
Of lesser danger: as, in politic bodies,
There's nothing more doth overwhelm the judgment,
And cloud the understanding, than too much
Settling and fixing, and, as 't were, subsiding
Upon one object. For the incorporating
Of these same outward things, into that part
Which we call mental, leaves some certain faeces
That stop the organs, and, as Plato says,
Assassinate our knowledge.

VOLP.   [*Aside.*] Now, the spirit
Of patience help me!

LADY P.   Come, in faith, I must
Visit you more a days; and make you well:
Laugh and be lusty.

VOLP. [*Aside.*] My good angel save me!

LADY P. There was but one sole man in all the world
With whom I e'er could sympathise; and he
Would lie[7] you, often, three, four hours together
To hear me speak; and be sometime so rapt,
As he would answer me quite from the purpose,
Like you, and you are like him, just. I'll discourse,
An 't be but only, sir, to bring you asleep,

7. *Would lie you*] Would often lie.

How we did spend our time and loves together,
For some six years.

VOLP.   Oh, oh, oh, oh, oh, oh!
LADY P. For we were coaetanei,[8] and brought up —
VOLP.   Some power, some fate, some fortune rescue me!

SCENE V. — *The same*

To them enter MOSCA.

MOS.   God save you, madam!
LADY P.   Good sir.
VOLP.   Mosca! welcome,
Welcome to my redemption.
MOS.   Why, sir?
VOLP.   Oh,
Rid me of this my torture, quickly, there;
My madam with the everlasting voice:
The bells, in time of pestilence, ne'er made
Like noise, or were in that perpetual motion!
The Cock-pit comes not near it. All my house,
But now, steam'd like a bath with her thick breath,
A lawyer could not have been heard; nor scarce
Another woman, such a hail of words
She has let fall. For hell's sake, rid her hence.
MOS.   Has she presented?
VOLP.   Oh, I do not care;
I'll take her absence upon any price,
With any loss.
MOS.   Madam —
LADY P.   I ha' brought your patron
A toy, a cap here, of mine own work.
MOS.   'T is well.
I had forgot to tell you I saw your knight
Where you would little think it. —
LADY P.   Where?

8. *coaetanei*] of the same age.

MOS.   Marry,
        Where yet, if you make haste, you may apprehend him,
        Rowing upon the water in a gondole,
        With the most cunning courtesan of Venice.
LADY P. Is 't true?
MOS.   Pursue 'em, and believe your eyes:
        Leave me to make your gift.
                                              [*Exit* LADY P. *hastily.*]
                              I knew 't would take:
        For, lightly, they that use themselves most licence,
        Are still most jealous.
VOLP.   Mosca, hearty thanks
        For thy quick fiction, and delivery of me.
        Now to my hopes, what sayst thou?

[*Re-enter* LADY P. WOULD-BE.]

LADY P.   But do you hear, sir? —
VOLP.   Again! I fear a paroxysm.
LADY P.   Which way
        Row'd they together?
MOS.   Toward the Rialto.
LADY P. I pray you lend me your dwarf.
MOS.   I pray you take him.   [*Exit* LADY P.]
        Your hopes, sir, are like happy blossoms, fair,
        And promise timely fruit, if you will stay
        But the maturing; keep you at your couch,
        Corbaccio will arrive straight, with the will;
        When he is gone, I'll tell you more.   [*Exit.*]
VOLP.   My blood,
        My spirits are return'd; I am alive:
        And, like your wanton gamester at primero,[1]
        Whose thought had whisper'd to him, not go less,
        Methinks I lie, and draw — for an encounter.

---

1. *not go less . . . encounter*] primero was the early form of the card game ombre; "go less,"
   "draw" and "encounter" are phrases used in the game.

SCENE VI. — *The same*

Enter MOSCA, BONARIO.

MOS. Sir, here conceal'd [*Opening a door*] you may hear all. But,
        pray you,
        Have patience, sir; [*One knocks.*] the same 's your father
        knocks:
        I am compell'd to leave you.   [*Exit.*]
BON.   Do so. — Yet
        Cannot my thought imagine this a truth.   [*Goes in.*]

SCENE VII. — *The same*

Enter MOSCA, CORVINO, CELIA. —

MOS. Death on me! you are come too soon, what meant you?
        Did not I say I would send?
CORV.   Yes, but I fear'd
        You might forget it, and then they prevent us.
MOS. Prevent! [*Aside.*] Did e'er man haste so for his horns?
        A courtier would not ply it so for a place.
        — Well, now there is no helping it, stay here;
        I'll presently return.
                                                        [*Exit.*]
CORV.   Where are you, Celia?
        You know not wherefore I have brought you hither?
CEL. Not well, except you told me.
CORV.   Now I will:
        Hark hither.
                                        [*They retire to one side.*]

[*Re-enter* MOSCA.]

MOS. (*to* BONARIO) Sir, your father hath sent word,

It will be half an hour ere he come;
And therefore, if you please to walk the while
Into that gallery — at the upper end,
There are some books to entertain the time:
And I'll take care no man shall come unto you, sir.

BON.   Yes. I will stay there. — [*Aside.*] I do doubt this fellow. [*Exit.*]
MOS.   [*Looking after him.*] There; he is far enough; he can hear
          nothing:
And for his father, I can keep him off.

[*Goes to* VOLPONE'S *couch, opens the curtains, and whispers to him.*]

CORV.   Nay, now, there is no starting back, and therefore,
Resolve upon it: I have so decreed.
It must be done. Nor would I move 't afore,
Because I would avoid all shifts and tricks,
That might deny me.
CEL.   Sir, let me beseech you,
Affect not these strange trials; if you doubt
My chastity, why, lock me up for ever;
Make me the heir of darkness. Let me live
Where I may please your fears, if not your trust.
CORV.   Believe it, I have no such humour, I.
All that I speak I mean; yet I'm not mad;
Not horn-mad, you see? Go to, show yourself
Obedient, and a wife.
CEL.   O heaven!
CORV.   I say it,
Do so.
CEL.   Was this the train?[1]
CORV.   I've told you reasons;
What the physicians have set down; how much
It may concern me; what my engagements are;
My means, and the necessity of those means
For my recovery: wherefore, if you be
Loyal and mine, be won, respect my venture.
CEL.   Before your honour?
CORV.   Honour! tut, a breath:

1. *"Was this the train?"*] "Was this what you had in mind all the time?"

There's no such thing in nature; a mere term
Invented to awe fools. What is my gold
The worse for touching, clothes for being look'd on?
Why, this 's no more. An old decrepit wretch,
That has no sense, no sinew; takes his meat
With others' fingers: only knows to gape
When you do scald his gums; a voice, a shadow;
And what can this man hurt you?

CEL. 　　　　　　　　[*Aside.*] Lord! what spirit
Is this hath ent'red him?

CORV. 　　　　　　　　And for your fame,
That's such a jig; as if I would go tell it,
Cry it on the Piazza! Who shall know it
But he that cannot speak it, and this fellow,
Whose lips are i' my pocket? Save yourself,
(If you'll proclaim 't, you may,) I know no other
Should come to know it.

CEL. 　Are heaven and saints then nothing?
Will they be blind or stupid?

CORV. 　　　　　　　　　How!

CEL. 　　　　　　　　　　Good sir,
Be jealous still, emulate them; and think
What hate they burn with toward every sin.

CORV. 　I grant you: if I thought it were a sin
I would not urge you. Should I offer this
To some young Frenchman, or hot Tuscan blood
That had read Aretine, conn'd all his prints,
Knew every quirk within lust's labyrinth,
And were profest critic in lechery;
And I would look upon him, and applaud him,
This were a sin: but here, 't is contrary,
A pious work, mere charity for physic,
And honest polity, to assure mine own.

CEL. 　O heaven! canst thou suffer such a change?

VOLP. 　Thou art mine honour, Mosca, and my pride,
My joy, my tickling, my delight! Go bring 'em.

MOS. 　[*Advancing.*] Please you draw near, sir.

CORV. 　　　　　　　　　　Come on, what—
You will not be rebellious? By that light—

MOS.   Sir, Signior Corvino, here, is come to see you.
VOLP.   Oh!
MOS.   And hearing of the consultation had,
          So lately, for your health, is come to offer,
          Or rather, sir, to prostitute —
CORV.   Thanks, sweet Mosca.
MOS.   Freely, unask'd, or unintreated —
CORV.   Well.
MOS.   As the true fervent instance of his love,
          His own most fair and proper wife; the beauty
          Only of price in Venice —
CORV.   'T is well urg'd.
MOS.   To be your comfortress, and to preserve you.
VOLP.   Alas, I am past, already! Pray you, thank him
          For his good care and promptness; but for that,
          'T is a vain labour e'en to fight 'gainst heaven;
          Applying fire to stone — uh, uh, uh, uh!

                                              [Coughing.]

          Making a dead leaf grow again. I take
          His wishes gently, though; and you may tell him
          What I have done for him: marry, my state is hopeless.
          Will him to pray for me; and to use his fortune
          With reverence when he comes to 't.
MOS.   Do you hear, sir?
          Go to him with your wife.
CORV   Heart of my father!
          Wilt thou persist thus? Come, I pray thee, come.
          Thou seest 't is nothing, Celia. By this hand
          I shall grow violent. Come, do 't, I say.
CEL.   Sir, kill me, rather: I will take down poison,
          Eat burning coals, do anything —
CORV.   Be damn'd!
          Heart, I will drag thee hence home by the hair;
          Cry thee a strumpet through the streets; rip up
          Thy mouth unto thine ears; and slit thy nose,
          Like a raw rochet![2] — Do not tempt me; come,
          Yield, I am loth — Death! I will buy some slave
          Whom I will kill, and bind thee to him alive;

2. *rochet*] a kind of fish.

And at my windore hang you forth, devising
Some monstrous crime, which I, in capital letters,
Will eat into thy flesh with aquafortis,
And burning cor'sives,[3] on this stubborn breast.
Now, by the blood thou hast incens'd, I'll do it!

CEL.   Sir, what you please, you may; I am your martyr.

CORV. Be not thus obstinate, I ha' not deserv'd it:
Think who it is intreats you. Prithee, sweet;—
Good faith, thou shalt have jewels, gowns, attires,
What thou wilt think, and ask. Do but go kiss him.
Or touch him but. For my sake. At my suit—
This once. No! not! I shall remember this.
Will you disgrace me thus? Do you thirst my undoing?

MOS.   Nay, gentle lady, be advis'd.

CORV.   No, no.
She has watch'd her time. God's precious, this is scurvy,
'T is very scurvy; and you are—

MOS.   Nay, good sir.

CORV. An arrant locust—by heaven, a locust!—
Whore, crocodile, that hast thy tears prepar'd,
Expecting how thou 'lt bid 'em flow—

MOS.   Nay, pray you, sir!
She will consider.

CEL.   Would my life would serve
To satisfy—

CORV. 'Sdeath! if she would but speak to him,
And save my reputation, 't were somewhat;
But spitefully to affect my utter ruin!

MOS.   Ay, now you have put your fortune in her hands.
Why i' faith, it is her modesty, I must quit her.
If you were absent, she would be more coming;
I know it: and dare undertake for her.
What woman can before her husband? Pray you,
Let us depart and leave her here.

CORV.   Sweet Celia,
Thou mayest redeem all yet; I'll say no more:
If not, esteem yourself as lost. Nay, stay there.

                                        [*Exit with* MOSCA.]

---

3. *aquafortis . . . cor'sives*] acids and corrosives.

CEL.   O God, and his good angels! whither, whither,
         Is shame fled human breasts? that with such ease,
         Men dare put off your honours, and their own?
         Is that, which ever was a cause of life,
         Now plac'd beneath the basest circumstance,
         And modesty an exile made, for money?

VOLP. Ay, in Corvino, and such earth-fed minds,
                               [*He leaps from his couch.*]
         That never tasted the true heaven of love.
         Assure thee, Celia, he that would sell thee,
         Only for hope of gain, and that uncertain,
         He would have sold his part of Paradise
         For ready money, had he met a cope-man.[4]
         Why art thou maz'd to see me thus reviv'd?
         Rather applaud thy beauty's miracle;
         'T is thy great work, that hath, not now alone,
         But sundry times rais'd me, in several shapes,
         And, but this morning, like a mountebank,
         To see thee at thy windore: ay, before
         I would have left my practice, for thy love,
         In varying figures, I would have contended
         With the blue Proteus, or the horned flood.[5]
         Now art thou welcome.

CEL.   Sir!

VOLP.   Nay, fly me not,
         Nor let thy false imagination
         That I was bed-rid, make thee think I am so:
         Thou shalt not find it. I am now as fresh,
         As hot, as high, and in as jovial plight
         As, when, in that so celebrated scene,
         At recitation of our comedy,
         For entertainment of the great Valois,[6]
         I acted young Antinous; and attracted
         The eyes and ears of all the ladies present,
         To admire each graceful gesture, note, and footing. [*Sings.*]

---

4. *cope-man*] buyer, merchant.
5. *blue Proteus, or the horned flood*] Proteus was a sea god who could take any shape at will; horned flood refers to the river god Achelous, who fought with Hercules, first in the shape of a river, then as a snake, then as a bull — hence "horned flood."
6. *Valois*] Henry of Valois, Duke of Anjou, the newly crowned King Henry III of France, was entertained with splendid festivities when he visited Venice in 1574.

Song[7]

> Come, my Celia, let us prove
> While we can, the sports of love,
> Time will not be ours for ever,
> He, at length, our good will sever;
> Spend not then his gifts in vain:
> Suns that set may rise again;
> But if once we lose this light,
> 'T is with us perpetual night.
> Why should we defer our joys?
> Fame and rumour are but toys.
> Cannot we delude the eyes
> Of a few poor household spies?
> Or his easier ears beguile,
> Thus removed by our wile?
> 'T is no sin love's fruits to steal;
> But the sweet thefts to reveal:
> To be taken, to be seen,
> These have crimes accounted been.

CEL.   Some serene[8] blast me, or dire lightning strike
        This my offending face!

VOLP.   Why droops my Celia?
        Thou hast, in place of a base husband found
        A worthy lover: use thy fortune well,
        With secrecy and pleasure. See, behold,
        What thou art queen of; not in expectation,
        As I feed others: but possess'd and crown'd.
        See, here, a rope of pearl; and each more orient
        Than the brave Aegyptian queen carous'd:
        Dissolve and drink 'em.[9] See, a carbuncle,
        May put out both the eyes of our St. Mark;
        A diamond would have bought Lollia Paulina,[10]
        When she came in like star-light, hid with jewels
        That were the spoils of provinces; take these
        And wear, and lose 'em; yet remains an earring
        To purchase them again, and this whole state.

7. The opening lines of the song are taken from Catullus.
8. *serene*] mist from heaven; malignant influence.
9. *Aegyptian queen ... drink 'em*] Supposedly, Cleopatra dissolved a precious pearl in wine, which she and Antony drank at a banquet.
10. *Lollia Paulina*] the wife of a Roman governor famed for the brilliance and costliness of her jewels.

A gem but worth a private patrimony
Is nothing; we will eat such at a meal.
The heads of parrots, tongues of nightingales,
The brains of peacocks, and of estriches,
Shall be our food, and, could we get the phoenix,
Though nature lost her kind, she were our dish.

CEL.   Good sir, these things might move a mind affected
With such delights; but I, whose innocence
Is all I can think wealthy, or worth th' enjoying,
And which, once lost, I have nought to lose beyond it,
Cannot be taken with these sensual baits:
If you have conscience —

VOLP.   'T is the beggar's virtue;
If thou hast wisdom, hear me, Celia.
Thy baths shall be the juice of July-flowers,
Spirit of roses, and of violets,
The milk of unicorns, and panthers' breath
Gather'd in bags, and mix'd with Cretan wines.
Our drink shall be prepared gold and amber;
Which we will take until my roof whirl round
With the vertigo: and my dwarf shall dance,
My eunuch sing, my fool make up the antic,
Whilst we, in changed shapes, act Ovid's tales,
Thou, like Europa now, and I like Jove,
Then I like Mars, and thou like Erycine:
So of the rest, till we have quite run through,
And wearied all the fables of the gods.
Then will I have thee in more modern forms,
Attired like some sprightly dame of France,
Brave Tuscan lady, or proud Spanish beauty;
Sometimes unto the Persian sophy's[11] wife;
Or the grand signior's mistress; and for change,
To one of our most artful courtesans,
Or some quick Negro, or cold Russian;
And I will meet thee in as many shapes:
Where we may so transfuse our wand'ring souls
Out at our lips, and score up sums of pleasures,

                                                            [*Sings.*]

11. *Persian sophy*] the Shah of Persia.

That the curious shall not know
How to tell them as they flow;
And the envious, when they find
What their number is, be pin'd.

CEL.   If you have ears that will be pierc'd — or eyes
That can be open'd — a heart that may be touch'd —
Or any part that yet sounds man about you —
If you have touch of holy saints — or heaven —
Do me the grace to let me scape: — if not,
Be bountiful and kill me. You do know,
I am a creature, hither ill betray'd,
By one whose shame I would forget it were:
If you will deign me neither of these graces,
Yet feed your wrath, sir, rather than your lust,
(It is a vice comes nearer manliness,)
And punish that unhappy crime of nature,
Which you miscall my beauty: flay my face,
Or poison it with ointments for seducing
Your blood to this rebellion. Rub these hands
With what may cause an eating leprosy,
E'en to my bones and marrow: anything
That may disfavour me, save in my honour —
And I will kneel to you, pray for you, pay down
A thousand hourly vows, sir, for your health;
Report, and think you virtuous —

VOLP.   Think me cold,
Frozen, and impotent, and so report me?
That I had Nestor's hernia,[12] thou wouldst think.
I do degenerate, and abuse my nation,
To play with opportunity thus long;
I should have done the act, and then have parley'd.
Yield, or I'll force thee.   [Seizes her.]

CEL.   O! just God!
VOLP.   In vain —
BON.   (leaps out from where MOSCA had placed him.) Forbear, foul
        ravisher! libidinous swine!
Free the forc'd lady, or thou diest, impostor.

---

12. *Nestor's hernia*] from Juvenal's sixth satire; senile impotence.

        But that I'm loth to snatch thy punishment
        Out of the hand of justice, thou shouldst yet
        Be made the timely sacrifice of vengeance,
        Before this altar and this dross, thy idol. —
        Lady, let's quit the place, it is the den
        Of villany; fear nought, you have a guard:
        And he ere long shall meet his just reward.

                                    [*Exeunt* BON. *and* CEL.]

VOLP.   Fall on me, roof, and bury me in ruin!
        Become my grave, that wert my shelter! O!
        I am unmask'd, unspirited, undone,
        Betray'd to beggary, to infamy —

SCENE VIII. — *The same*

VOLPONE. *Enter* MOSCA, *wounded and bleeding*.

MOS.   Where shall I run, most wretched shame of men,
        To beat out my unlucky brains?
VOLP.   Here, here.
        What! dost thou bleed?
MOS.   O, that his well-driv'n sword
        Had been so courteous to have cleft me down
        Unto the navel, ere I liv'd to see
        My life, my hopes, my spirits, my patron, all
        Thus desperately engaged by my error!
VOLP.   Woe on thy fortune!
MOS.   And my follies, sir.
VOLP.   Thou hast made me miserable.
MOS.   And myself, sir.
        Who would have thought he would have heark'ned so?
VOLP.   What shall we do?
MOS.   I know not; if my heart
        Could expiate the mischance, I'd pluck it out.
        Will you be pleas'd to hang me, or cut my throat?
        And I'll requite you, sir. Let 's die like Romans,[1]

---

1. *die like Romans*] i.e., by suicide.

Since we have liv'd like Grecians.

They knock without.

VOLP.   Hark! who's there?
I hear some footing; officers, the saffi,[2]
Come to apprehend us! I do feel the brand
Hissing already at my forehead; now
Mine ears are boring.

MOS.   To your couch, sir, you,
Make that place good, however. [VOLPONE *lies down as before.*] Guilty men
Suspect what they deserve still. Signior Corbaccio!

SCENE IX. — *The same*

To them enter CORBACCIO.

CORB.   Why, how now, Mosca?
MOS.   O, undone, amaz'd, sir.
Your son, I know not by what accident,
Acquainted with your purpose to my patron,
Touching your will, and making him your heir,
Ent'red our house with violence, his sword drawn,
Sought for you, called you wretch, unnatural,
Vow'd he would kill you.

CORB.   Me!
MOS.   Yes, and my patron.
CORB.   This act shall disinherit him indeed:
Here is the will.
MOS.   'T is well, sir.
CORB.   Right and well:
Be you as careful now for me.

[*Enter* VOLTORE *behind.*]

MOS.   My life, sir,
Is not more tender'd; I am only yours.

_____

2. *saffi*] bailiff's attendants.

CORB.   How does he? Will he die shortly, think'st thou?
MOS.   I fear
He'll outlast May.
CORB.   To-day?
MOS.   No, last out May, sir.
CORB.   Couldst thou not gi' him a dram?
MOS.   O, by no means, sir.
CORB.   Nay, I'll not bid you.
VOLT.   [*coming forward.*] This is a knave, I see.
MOS.   [*Aside, seeing* VOLT.] How! Signior Voltore! did he hear me?
VOLT.   Parasite!
MOS.   Who's that? — O, sir, most timely welcome —
VOLT.   Scarce,
To the discovery of your tricks, I fear.
You are his, *only*? And mine also, are you not?
MOS.   Who? I, sir!
VOLT.   You, sir. What device is this
About a will?
MOS.   A plot for you, sir.
VOLT.   Come,
Put not your foists[1] upon me; I shall scent 'em.
MOS.   Did you not hear it?
VOLT.   Yes, I hear Corbaccio
Hath made your patron there his heir.
MOS.   'T is true,
By my device, drawn to it by my plot,
With hope —
VOLT.   Your patron should reciprocate?
And you have promis'd?
MOS.   For your good I did, sir.
Nay, more, I told his son, brought, hid him here,
Where he might hear his father pass the deed;
Being persuaded to it by this thought, sir,
That the unnaturalness, first, of the act,
And then his father's oft disclaiming in him,
(Which I did mean t' help on), would sure enrage him
To do some violence upon his parent,
On which the law should take sufficient hold,
And you be stated in a double hope.

---

1. *foists*] tricks, deceits, but also bad smells.

	Truth be my comfort, and my conscience,
	My only aim was to dig you a fortune
	Out of these two rotten sepulchres —
VOLT.	I cry thee mercy, Mosca.
MOS.	— Worth your patience,
	And your great merit, sir. And see the change!
VOLT.	Why, what success?
MOS.	Most hapless! you must help, sir.

VOLT. I cry thee mercy, Mosca.

MOS.   — Worth your patience,
       And your great merit, sir. And see the change!

VOLT. Why, what success?

MOS.   Most hapless! you must help, sir.
       Whilst we expected th' old raven, in comes
       Corvino's wife, sent hither by her husband —

VOLT. What, with a present?

MOS.   No, sir, on visitation;
       (I'll tell you how anon;) and staying long,
       The youth he grows impatient, rushes forth,
       Seizeth the lady, wounds me, makes her swear
       (Or he would murder her, that was his vow)
       T' affirm my patron to have done her rape:
       Which how unlike it is, you see! and hence,
       With that pretext he's gone, t' accuse his father,
       Defame my patron, defeat you —

VOLT.   Where 's her husband?
       Let him be sent for straight.

MOS.   Sir, I'll go fetch him.

VOLT. Bring him to the Scrutineo.[2]

MOS.   Sir, I will.

VOLT. This must be stopt.

MOS.   O you do nobly, sir.
       Alas, 't was labour'd all, sir, for your good;
       Nor was there want of counsel in the plot:
       But Fortune can, at any time, o'erthrow
       The projects of a hundred learned clerks, sir.

CORB. [listening.] What 's that?

VOLT.   Wilt please you, sir, to go along?
                    [Exit CORBACCIO, followed by VOLTORE.]

MOS.   Patron, go in, and pray for our success.

VOLP. [rising from his couch.] Need makes devotion: heaven your
       labour bless!
                                        [Exeunt.]

---

2. *Scrutineo*] Senate House, or court of law.

ACT IV

SCENE I. — *A street*

Enter SIR POLITIC WOULD-BE, PEREGRINE.

SIR P.   I told you, sir, it was a plot; you see
What observation is! You mention'd[1] me
For some instructions: I will tell you, sir,
(Since we are met here in this height of Venice,)
Some few particulars I have set down,
Only for this meridian, fit to be known
Of your crude traveller; and they are these.
I will not touch, sir, at your phrase, or clothes,
For they are old.

PER.   Sir, I have better.

SIR P.   Pardon,
I meant, as they are themes.

PER.   O, sir, proceed:
I'll slander you no more of wit, good sir.

SIR P.   First, for your garb,[2] it must be grave and serious,
Very reserv'd and lockt; not tell a secret
On any terms, not to your father; scarce
A fable, but with caution: make sure choice
Both of your company and discourse; beware
You never speak a truth —

PER.   How!

SIR P.   Not to strangers,
For those be they you must converse with most;

---

1. *mention'd*] asked.
2. *garb*] bearing, demeanor.

	Others I would not know, sir, but at distance

Others I would not know, sir, but at distance
So as I still might be a saver in them:
You shall have tricks else past upon you hourly.
And then, for your religion, profess none,
But wonder at the diversity of all;
And, for your part, protest, were there no other
But simply the laws o' th' land, you could content you.
Nic. Machiavel and Monsieur Bodin,[3] both
Were of this mind. Then must you learn the use
And handling of your silver fork at meals,
The metal of your glass; (these are main matters
With your Italian;) and to know the hour
When you must eat your melons and your figs.

PER.   Is that a point of state too?

SIR P.   Here it is:
For your Venetian, if he see a man
Preposterous in the least, he has him straight;
He has; he strips him. I'll acquaint you, sir.
I now have liv'd here 't is some fourteen months:
Within the first week of my landing here,
All took me for a citizen of Venice,
I knew the forms so well —

PER.   [Aside.]   And nothing else.

SIR P.   I had read Contarene,[4] took me a house,
Dealt with my Jews to furnish it with movables —
Well, if I could but find one man, one man
To mine own heart, whom I durst trust, I would —

PER.   What, what, sir?

SIR P.   Make him rich; make him a fortune:
He should not think again. I would command it.

PER.   As how?

SIR P.   With certain projects that I have;
Which I may not discover.[5]

PER.   [Aside.]   If I had

---

3. *Nic. Machiavel . . . Bodin*] Niccolò Machiavelli (1469–1527), the Italian statesman,
politician and philosopher, and Jean Bodin, a French political philosopher, who advo-
cated religious tolerance.
4. *Contarene*] Contarini, author of a book on Venetian government.
5. *discover*] disclose, reveal.

But one to wager with, I would lay odds now,
He tells me instantly.

Sir P.   One is, and that
I care not greatly who knows, to serve the state
Of Venice with red herrings for three years,
And at a certain rate, from Rotterdam,
Where I have correspondence. There 's a letter,
Sent me from one o' th' states, and to that purpose:
He cannot write his name, but that's his mark.

Per.   He is a chandler?

Sir P.   No, a cheesemonger.
There are some others too with whom I treat
About the same negotiation;
And I will undertake it: for 't is thus.
I'll do 't with ease, I have cast it all. Your hoy[6]
Carries but three men in her, and a boy;
And she shall make me three returns a year:
So if there come but one of three, I save;
If two, I can defalk:[7] — but this is now,
If my main project fail.

Per.   Then you have others?

Sir P.   I should be loth to draw the subtle air
Of such a place, without my thousand aims.
I'll not dissemble, sir: where'er I come,
I love to be considerative; and 't is true,
I have at my free hours thought upon
Some certain goods unto the state of Venice,
Which I do call my Cautions; and, sir, which
I mean, in hope of pension, to propound
To the Great Council, then unto the Forty,
So to the Ten.[8] My means are made already —

Per.   By whom?

Sir P.   Sir, one that though his place be obscure,
Yet he can sway, and they will hear him. He 's
A *commandadore*.

Per.   What! a common serjeant?

Sir P.   Sir, such as they are, put it in their mouths,

---

6. *hoy*] a small passenger sloop.
7. *defalk*] cut off, reduce.
8. *Great Council . . . the Ten*] increasingly lofty legislative bodies of the Venetian government.

What they should say, sometimes; as well as greater:
I think I have my notes to show you —

                              [*Searching his pockets.*]

PER.   Good sir.
SIR P. But you shall swear unto me, on your gentry,
Not to anticipate —
PER.   I, sir!
SIR P.   Nor reveal
A circumstance — My paper is not with me.
PER. O, but you can remember, sir.
SIR P.   My first is
Concerning tinder-boxes. You must know,
No family is here without its box.
Now, sir, it being so portable a thing,
Put case, that you or I were ill affected
Unto the state, sir; with it in our pockets,
Might not I go into the Arsenal,
Or you come out again, and none the wiser?
PER. Except yourself, sir.
SIR P.   Go to, then. I therefore
Advertise to the state, how fit it were
That none but such as were known patriots,
Sound lovers of their country, should be suffer'd
T' enjoy them in their houses; and even those
Seal'd at some office, and at such a bigness
As might not lurk in pockets.
PER.   Admirable!
SIR P. My next is, how t' inquire, and be resolv'd
By present demonstration, whether a ship,
Newly arriv'd from Soria,[9] or from
Any suspected part of all the Levant,[10]
Be guilty of the plague: and where they use
To lie out forty, fifty days, sometimes,
About the Lazaretto, for their trial;
I'll save that charge and loss unto the merchant,
And in an hour clear the doubt.
PER.   Indeed, sir!
SIR P. Or — I will lose my labour.

---

9. *Soria*] Syria.
10. *Levant*] Middle East.

PER.	My faith, that's much.
SIR P.	Nay, sir, conceive me. It will cost me in onions,
	Some thirty livres—
PER.	Which is one pound sterling.
SIR P.	Beside my waterworks: for this I do, sir.
	First, I bring in your ship 'twixt two brick walls;
	But those the state shall venture. On the one
	I strain me a fair tarpauling, and in that
	I stick my onions, cut in halves; the other
	Is full of loopholes, out of which I thrust
	The noses of my bellows; and those bellows
	I keep, with waterworks, in perpetual motion,
	Which is the easiest matter of a hundred.
	Now, sir, your onion, which doth naturally
	Attract th' infection, and your bellows blowing
	The air upon him, will show instantly,
	By his chang'd colour, if there be contagion;
	Or else remain as fair as at the first.
	Now it is known, 't is nothing.
PER.	You are right, sir.
SIR P.	I would I had my note.
PER.	Faith, so would I:
	But you ha' done well for once, sir.
SIR P.	Were I false,
	Or would be made so, I could show you reasons
	How I could sell this state now to the Turk,
	Spite of their galleys, or their—
	[*Examining his papers.*]
PER.	Pray you, Sir Pol.
SIR P.	I have 'em not about me.
PER.	That I fear'd.
	They are there, sir?
SIR P.	No, this is my diary,
	Wherein I note my actions of the day.
PER.	Pray you let 's see, sir. What is here? *Notandum*,[11] [*Reads.*]
	"A rat had gnawn my spur-leathers; notwithstanding,
	I put on new, and did go forth; but first
	I threw three beans over the threshold. Item,

---

11. Notandum] take special note.

I went and bought two toothpicks, whereof one
I burst immediately, in a discourse
With a Dutch merchant, 'bout *ragion' del stato*.[12]
From him I went and paid a *moccinigo*
For piecing my silk stockings; by the way
I cheapen'd[13] sprats; and at St. Mark's I urin'd."
'Faith these are politic notes!

SIR P.   Sir, I do slip
No action of my life, but thus I quote[14] it.

PER.   Believe me, it is wise!

SIR P.   Nay, sir, read forth.

SCENE II. — *The same*

Enter, at a distance, LADY POLITIC WOULD-BE, NANO, 2 *Waiting-
women.*

LADY P. Where should this loose knight be, trow? Sure he's hous'd.

NAN.   Why, then he's fast.

LADY P.   Ay, he plays both[1] with me.
I pray you stay. This heat will do more harm
To my complexion than his heart is worth.
(I do not care to hinder, but to take him.)
How it comes off!   [*Rubbing her cheeks.*]

1ST WOM.   My master's yonder.

LADY P.   Where?

2ND WOM.   With a young gentleman.

LADY P.   That same's the party:
In man's apparel! Pray you, sir, jog my knight:
I will be tender to his reputation,
However he demerit.

12. *ragion' del stato*] "reason of state," politics.
13. *cheapen'd*] bargained for.
14. *quote*] note.

1. *he plays both*] both "fast and loose."

SIR P.	[*seeing her.*] My lady!
PER.	Where?
SIR P.	'T is she indeed, sir; you shall know her. She is,
	Were she not mine, a lady of that merit,
	For fashion and behaviour; and for beauty
	I durst compare —
PER.	It seems you are not jealous,
	That dare commend her.
SIR P.	Nay, and for discourse —
PER.	Being your wife, she cannot miss that.
SIR P.	[*introducing Per.*] Madam,
	Here is a gentleman, pray you, use him fairly;
	He seems a youth, but he is —
LADY P.	None.
SIR P.	Yes one
	Has put his face as soon into the world —
LADY P.	You mean, as early? But to-day?
SIR P.	How's this?
LADY P.	Why, in this habit, sir; you apprehend me.
	Well, Master Would-be, this doth not become you;
	I had thought the odour, sir, of your good name
	Had been more precious to you; that you would not
	Have done this dire massacre on your honour;
	One of your gravity, and rank besides!
	But knights, I see, care little for the oath
	They make to ladies; chiefly their own ladies.
SIR P.	Now, by my spurs, the symbol of my knighthood —
PER.	[*Aside.*] Lord, how his brain is humbl'd for an oath!
SIR P.	I reach[2] you not.
LADY P.	Right, sir, your polity
	May bear it through thus. Sir, a word with you.

[*To* PER.]

I would be loth to contest publicly
With any gentlewoman, or to seem
Froward, or violent, as the courtier says;
It comes too near rusticity in a lady,
Which I would shun by all means: and however

2. *reach*] understand.

<pre>
                I may deserve from Master Would-be, yet
                T' have one fair gentlewoman thus be made
                The unkind instrument to wrong another,
                And one she knows not, ay, and to perséver;
                In my poor judgment, is not warranted
                From being a solecism in our sex,
                If not in manners.
PER.   How is this!
SIR P.   Sweet madam,
                Come nearer to your aim.
LADY P.   Marry, and will, sir.
                Since you provoke me with your impudence,
                And laughter of your light land-syren here,
                Your Sporus,[3] your hermaphrodite —
PER.   What 's here?
                Poetic fury and historic storms!
SIR P.   The gentleman, believe it, is of worth
                And of our nation.
LADY P.   Ay, your Whitefriars nation.[4]
                Come, I blush for you, Master Would-be, I;
                And am asham'd you should ha' no more forehead
                Than thus to be the patron, or St. George,
                To a lewd harlot, a base fricatrice,[5]
                A female devil, in a male outside.
SIR P.   Nay,
                An you be such a one, I must bid adieu
                To your delights. The case appears too liquid.
                                                          [Exit.]

LADY P.   Ay, you may carry 't clear, with you state-face!
                But for your carnival concupiscence,
                Who here is fled for liberty of conscience,
                From furious persecution of the marshal,
                Her will I disc'ple.[6]
PER.   This is fine, i' faith!
                And do you use this often? Is this part
</pre>

3. *Sporus*] one of Nero's favorite catamites, whom he dressed in drag and married.
4. *Whitefriars nation*] a disreputable part of London, inhabited by prostitutes.
5. *fricatrice*] prostitute.
6. *disc'ple*] discipline.

Of your wit's exercise, 'gainst you have occasion?
Madam —
LADY P.　Go to, sir.
PER.　　　　　　　　Do you hear me, lady?
Why, if your knight have set you to beg shirts,
Or to invite me home, you might have done it
A nearer way by far.
LADY P.　　　　　　　　This cannot work you
Out of my snare.
PER.　　　　　　　　Why, am I in it, then?
Indeed your husband told me you were fair,
And so you are; only your nose inclines,
That side that 's next the sun, to the queen-apple.[7]
LADY P.　This cannot be endur'd by any patience.

SCENE III. — *The same*

To them enter MOSCA.

MOS.　What is the matter, madam?
LADY P.　　　　　　　　　If the senate
Right not my quest in this, I will protest 'em
To all the world no aristocracy.
MOS.　What is the injury, lady?
LADY P.　　　　　　　　Why, the callet[1]
You told me of, here I have ta'en disguis'd.
MOS.　Who? this! what means your ladyship? The creature
I mention'd to you is apprehended now,
Before the senate; you shall see her —
LADY P.　　　　　　　　　Where?
MOS.　I'll bring you to her. This young gentleman,
I saw him land this morning at the port.
LADY P.　Is 't possible! how has my judgment wander'd?

---

7. *your nose . . . queen-apple*] her nose is red.

---

1. *callet*] prostitute.

Sir, I must, blushing, say to you, I have err'd;
And plead your pardon.
PER.   What, more changes yet!
LADY P. I hope you ha' not the malice to remember
A gentlewoman's passion. If you stay
In Venice here, please you to use me, sir —
MOS.   Will you go, madam?
LADY P.   Pray you, sir, use me; in faith,
The more you see me the more I shall conceive
You have forgot our quarrel.
[*Exeunt* LADY WOULD-BE, MOSCA, NANO, *and* Waiting-women.]
PER.   This is rare!
Sir Politic Would-be? No, Sir Politic Bawd,
To bring me thus acquainted with his wife!
Well, wise Sir Pol, since you have practis'd thus
Upon my freshman-ship, I'll try your salt-head,[2]
What proof it is against a counter-plot.
                                        [*Exit.*]

SCENE IV. — *The Scrutineo*

Enter VOLTORE, CORBACCIO, CORVINO, MOSCA.

VOLT.   Well, now you know the carriage of the business,
Your constancy is all that is requir'd
Unto the safety of it.
MOS.   Is the lie
Safely convey'd amongst us? Is that sure?
Knows every man his burden?
CORV.   Yes.
MOS.   Then shrink not.
CORV.   But knows the advocate the truth?
MOS.   O, sir,
By no means; I devis'd a formal tale,
That salv'd your reputation. But be valiant, sir.

_____

2. *salt-head*] salaciousness, lasciviousness.

CORV.   I fear no one but him that this his pleading
          Should make him stand for a co-heir —

MOS.   Co-halter!
          Hang him; we will but use his tongue, his noise,
          As we do croaker's[1] here.

CORV.   Ay, what shall he do?

MOS.   When we ha' done, you mean?

CORV.   Yes.

MOS.   Why, we'll think;
          Sell him for mummia:[2] he's half dust already. —
          Do you not smile, (*to* VOLTORE) to see this buffalo,[3]
          How he doth sport it with his head? [*Aside.*] I should,
          If all were well and past. — Sir, (*to* CORBACCIO) only you
          Are he that shall enjoy the crop of all,
          And these not know for whom they toil.

CORB.   Ay, peace.

MOS.   (*turning to* CORVINO.) But you shall eat it. [*Aside.*] Much! —
            Worshipful sir, (*to* VOLTORE)
          Mercury sit upon your thund'ring tongue,
          Or the French Hercules, and make your language
          As conquering as his club, to beat along,
          As with a tempest, flat, our adversaries;
          But much more yours, sir.

VOLT.   Here they come, ha' done.

MOS.   I have another witness, if you need, sir,
          I can produce.

VOLT.   Who is it?

MOS.   Sir, I have her.

---

1. *croaker's*] Corbaccio's.
2. *mummia*] a medicine; supposedly made from the oozing from mummies.
3. *buffalo*] an allusion to a cuckold's horns.

SCENE V. — *The same*

Enter 4 Avocatori, *and take their seats*, BONARIO, CELIA, Notario, Commandadori, Saffi, *and other* Officers of Justice.

1ST AVOC.   The like of this the senate never heard of.

2ND AVOC.   'T will come most strange to them when we report it.

4TH AVOC.   The gentlewoman has been ever held
       Of unreproved name.

3RD AVOC.   So has the youth.

4TH AVOC.   The more unnatural part that of his father.

2ND AVOC.   More of the husband.

1ST AVOC.   I not know to give
       His act a name, it is so monstrous!

4TH AVOC.   But the impostor, he's a thing created.
       T' exceed example!

1ST AVOC.   And all after-times!

2ND AVOC.   I never heard a true voluptuary
       Describ'd but him.

3RD AVOC.   Appear yet those were cited?

NOT.   All but the old magnifico, Volpone.

1ST AVOC.   Why is not he here?

MOS.   Please your fatherhoods,
       Here is his advocate: himself's so weak,
       So feeble —

4TH AVOC.   Who are you?

BON.   His parasite,
       His knave, his pander. I beseech the court
       He may be forc'd to come, that your grave eyes
       May bear strong witness of his strange impostures.

VOLT.   Upon my faith and credit with your virtues.
       He is not able to endure the air.

2ND AVOC.   Bring him.

3RD AVOC.   We will see him.

4TH AVOC.   Fetch him.

VOLT.   Your fatherhoods' fit pleasures be obey'd;

                              [*Exeunt* Officers.]

But sure, the sight will rather move your pities
Than indignation. May it please the court,
In the mean time, he may be heard in me.
I know this place most void of prejudice,
And therefore crave it, since we have no reason
To fear our truth should hurt our cause.

3RD AVOC.   Speak free.

VOLT.   Then know, most honour'd fathers, I must now
Discover to your strangely abus'd ears,
The most prodigious and most frontless piece
Of solid impudence, and treachery,
That ever vicious nature yet brought forth
To shame the state of Venice. This lewd woman,
That wants no artificial looks or tears
To help the vizor she has now put on,
Hath long been known a close adulteress
To that lascivious youth there; not suspected,
I say, but known, and taken in the act
With him; and by this man, the easy husband,
Pardon'd; whose timeless bounty makes him now
Stand here, the most unhappy, innocent person,
That ever man's own goodness made accus'd.
For these not knowing how to owe a gift
Of that dear grace, but with their shame; being plac'd
So above all powers of their gratitude,
Began to hate the benefit; and in place
Of thanks, devise t' extirp the memory
Of such an act: wherein I pray your fatherhoods
To observe the malice, yea, the rage of creatures
Discover'd in their evils: and what heart
Such take, ev'n from their crimes: — but that anon
Will more appear. — This gentleman, the father,
Hearing of this foul fact, with many others,
Which daily struck at his too tender ears,
And griev'd in nothing more than that he could not
Preserve himself a parent (his son's ills
Growing to that strange flood), at last decreed
To disinherit him.

1ST AVOC.   These be strange turns!

2ND AVOC. The young man's fame was ever fair and honest.

VOLT.   So much more full of danger is his vice,
          That can beguile so, under shade of virtue.
          But, as I said, my honour'd sires, his father
          Having this settled purpose, by what means
          To him betray'd, we know not, and this day
          Appointed for the deed; that parricide,
          I cannot style him better, by confederacy
          Preparing this his paramour to be there,
          Ent'red Volpone's house (who was the man,
          Your fatherhoods must understand, design'd
          For the inheritance), there sought his father: —
          But with what purpose sought he him, my lords?
          I tremble to pronounce it, that a son
          Unto a father, and to such a father,
          Should have so foul, felonious intent!
          It was to murder him: when being prevented
          By his more happy absence, what then did he?
          Not check his wicked thoughts; no, now new deeds;
          (Mischief doth never end where it begins)
          An act of horror, fathers! He dragg'd forth
          The aged gentleman that had there lain bedrid
          Three years and more, out of his innocent couch,
          Naked upon the floor; there left him; wounded
          His servant in the face; and with this strumpet,
          The stale[1] to his forg'd practice, who was glad
          To be so active, — (I shall here desire
          Your fatherhoods to note but my collections,
          As most remarkable, —) thought at once to stop
          His father's ends, discredit his free choice
          In the old gentleman, redeem themselves,
          By laying infamy upon this man,
          To whom, with blushing, they should owe their lives.

1ST AVOC.   What proofs have you of this?
BON.   Most honour'd fathers,
          I humbly crave there be no credit given
          To this man's mercenary tongue.
2ND AVOC.   Forbear.
BON.   His soul moves in his fee.

---

1. *The stale*] The decoy.

3RD Avoc.   O, sir.
BON.   This fellow,
  For six sols[2] more would plead against his Maker.
1ST Avoc. You do forget yourself.
VOLT.   Nay, nay, grave fathers,
  Let him have scope: can any man imagine
  That he will spare his accuser, that would not
  Have spar'd his parent?
1ST Avoc.   Well, produce your proofs.
CEL. I would I could forget I were a creature.
VOLT. Signior Corbaccio!

             [CORBACCIO *comes forward.*]
4TH Avoc.   What is he?
VOLT.   The father.
2ND Avoc. Has he had an oath?
NOT. Yes.
CORB.   What must I do now?
NOT. Your testimony's crav'd.
CORB.   Speak to the knave?
  I'll ha' my mouth first stopt with earth; my heart
  Abhors his knowledge: I disclaim in[3] him.
1ST Avoc. But for what cause?
CORB.   The mere portent of nature!
  He is an utter stranger to my loins.
BON. Have they made you to this?
CORB.   I will not hear thee,
  Monster of men, swine, goat, wolf, parricide!
  Speak not, thou viper.
BON.   Sir, I will sit down,
  And rather wish my innocence should suffer
  Than I resist the authority of a father.
VOLT. Signior Corvino!

           [CORVINO *comes forward.*]
2ND Avoc.   This is strange.
1ST Avoc.   Who's this?
NOT. The husband.
4TH Avoc.   Is he sworn?

  2. *six sols*] three pence.
  3. *disclaim in him*] disown him.

NOT.	He is.
3RD AVOC.	Speak then.

CORV.   This woman, please your fatherhoods, is a whore,
Of most hot exercise, more than a partridge,
Upon record —

1ST AVOC.   No more.

CORV.   Neighs like a jennet.[4]

NOT.   Preserve the honour of the court.

CORV.   I shall,
And modesty of your most reverend ears.
And yet I hope that I may say, these eyes
Have seen her glu'd unto that piece of cedar,
That fine well timber'd gallant: and that here
The letters may be read, thorough the horn,[5]
That make the story perfect.

MOS.   Excellent! sir.

CORV.   [*Aside to* MOSCA.] There is no shame in this now, is there?

MOS.   None.

CORV.   Or if I said, I hop'd that she were onward
To her damnation, if there be a hell
Greater than whore and woman, a good Catholic
May make the doubt.

3RD AVOC.   His grief hath made him frantic.

1ST AVOC.   Remove him hence.

2ND AVOC.   Look to the woman.

          [CELIA *swoons.*]

CORV.   Rare!
Prettily feign'd again!

4TH AVOC.   Stand from about her.

1ST AVOC.   Give her the air.

3RD AVOC.   What can you say?   [*To* MOSCA.]

MOS.   My wound,
May it please your wisdoms, speaks for me, receiv'd
In aid of my good patron, when he mist
His sought-for father, when that well-taught dame
Had her cue giv'n her to cry out, "A rape!"

---

4. *jennet*] mare in heat.
5. *the horn*] of the cuckold.

BON.   O most laid[6] impudence! Fathers —
3RD AVOC.   Sir, be silent;
          You had your hearing free, so must they theirs.
2ND AVOC. I do begin to doubt th' imposture here.
4TH AVOC. This woman has too many moods.
VOLT.   Grave fathers,
          She is a creature of a most profest
          And prostituted lewdness.
CORV.   Most impetuous,
          Unsatisfi'd, grave fathers!
VOLT.   May her feignings
          Not take your wisdoms: but this day she baited
          A stranger, a grave knight, with her loose eyes,
          And more lascivious kisses. This man saw 'em
          Together on the water, in a gondola.
MOS.   Here is the lady herself, that saw them too,
          Without; who then had in the open streets
          Pursu'd them, but for saving her knight's honour.
1ST AVOC. Produce that lady.
2ND AVOC.   Let her come.   [*Exit* MOSCA.]
4TH AVOC.   These things,
          They strike with wonder.
3RD AVOC.   I am turn'd a stone.

SCENE VI. — *The same*

To them re-enter MOSCA *with* LADY WOULD-BE.

MOS.   Be resolute, madam.
LADY P.   Ay, this same is she.

                              [*Pointing to* CELIA.]
          Out, thou chameleon harlot! now thine eyes
          Vie tears with the hyena. Dar'st thou look
          Upon my wronged face? I cry your pardons,

    6. *laid*] well-contrived.

I fear I have forgettingly transgrest
Against the dignity of the court—
2ND AVOC.   No, madam.
LADY P.   And been exorbitant—
2ND AVOC.   You have not, lady.
4TH AVOC.   These proofs are strong.
LADY P.   Surely, I had no purpose
To scandalize your honours, or my sex's.
3RD AVOC.   We do believe it.
LADY P.   Surely you may believe it.
2ND AVOC.   Madam, we do.
LADY P.   Indeed you may; my breeding
Is not so coarse—
4TH AVOC.   We know it.
LADY P.   To offend
With pertinacy—
3RD AVOC.   Lady—
LADY P.   Such a presence!
No surely.
1ST AVOC.   We will think it.
LADY P.   You may think it.
1ST AVOC.   Let her o'ercome. What witnesses have you,
To make good your report?
BON.   Our consciences.
CEL.   And heaven, that never fails the innocent.
1ST AVOC.   These are no testimonies.
BON.   Not in your courts,
Where multitude and clamour overcomes.
1ST AVOC.   Nay, then you do wax insolent.

VOLPONE [*brought in, as impotent*].

VOLT.   Here, here,
The testimony comes that will convince,
And put to utter dumbness their bold tongues!
See here, grave fathers, here's the ravisher,
The rider on men's wives, the great impostor,
The grand voluptuary! Do you not think
These limbs should affect venery? or these eyes
Covet a concubine? Pray you mark these hands;

Are they not fit to stroke a lady's breasts?
Perhaps he doth dissemble!

BON. So he does.
VOLT. Would you ha' him tortur'd?
BON. I would have him prov'd.
VOLT. Best try him then with goads, or burning irons;
Put him to the strappado:[1] I have heard
The rack hath cur'd the gout; faith, give it him,
And help him of a malady; be courteous.
I'll undertake, before these honour'd fathers,
He shall have yet as many left diseases,
As she has known adulterers, or thou strumpets.
O, my most equal hearers, if these deeds,
Acts of this bold and most exorbitant strain,
May pass with suff'rance, what one citizen
But owes the forfeit of his life, yea, fame,
To him that dares traduce him? Which of you
Are safe, my honour'd fathers? I would ask,
With leave of your grave fatherhoods, if their plot
Have any face or colour like to truth?
Or if, unto the dullest nostril here,
It smell not rank, and most abhorred slander?
I crave your care of this good gentleman,
Whose life is much endanger'd by their fable;
And as for them, I will conclude with this,
That vicious persons, when they're hot, and flesh'd
In impious acts, their constancy[2] abounds:
Damn'd deeds are done with greatest confidence.

1ST AVOC. Take 'em to custody, and sever them.
2ND AVOC. 'T is pity two such prodigies should live.
1ST AVOC. Let the old gentleman be return'd with care.

[*Exeunt* Officers *with* VOLPONE.]

I'm sorry our credulity wrong'd him.
4TH AVOC. These are two creatures!

---

1. *strappado*] a form of torture in which a man's hands were tied behind his back and he was hoisted by his wrists on a gallows, the usual result being the dislocation of his shoulders.
2. *constancy*] boldness.

3RD AVOC.   I've an earthquake in me.

2ND AVOC.   Their shame, ev'n in their cradles, fled their faces.

4TH AVOC.   You have done a worthy service to the state, sir,
       In their discovery.   [*To* VOLT.]

1ST AVOC.   You shall hear, ere night,
       What punishment the court decrees upon 'em.
       [*Exeunt* Avocat., Not., *and* Officers *with* BONARIO *and*
        CELIA.]

VOLT.   We thank your fatherhoods. How like you it?

MOS.   Rare.
       I'd ha' your tongue, sir, tipt with gold for this;
       I'd ha' you be the heir to the whole city;
       The earth I'd have want men ere you want living:
       They're bound to erect your statue in St. Mark's.
       Signior Corvino, I would have you go
       And show yourself that you have conquer'd.

CORV.   Yes.

MOS.   It was much better that you should profess
       Yourself a cuckold thus, than that the other
       Should have been prov'd.

CORV.   Nay, I consider'd that:
       Now it is her fault.

MOS.   Then it had been yours.

CORV.   True; I do doubt this advocate still.

MOS.   I' faith.
       You need not, I dare ease you of that care.

CORV.   I trust thee, Mosca.   [*Exit.*]

MOS.   As your own soul, sir.

CORB.   Mosca!

MOS.   Now for your business, sir.

CORB.   How! ha' you business?

MOS.   Yes, yours, sir,

CORB.   O, none else?

MOS.   None else, not I.

CORB.   Be careful then.

MOS.   Rest you with both your eyes, sir.

CORB.   Dispatch it.

MOS.   Instantly.

CORB.   And look that all,

	Whatever, be put in, jewels, plate, moneys,
	Household stuff, bedding, curtains.
Mos.	Curtain-rings, sir:
	Only the advocate's fee must be deducted.
Corb.	I'll pay him now; you'll be too prodigal.
Mos.	Sir, I must tender it.
Corb.	Two chequins is well.
Mos.	No, six, sir.
Corb.	'T is too much.
Mos.	He talk'd a great while;
	You must consider that, sir.
Corb.	Well, there's three —
Mos.	I'll give it him.
Corb.	Do so, and there's for thee. 　　　　　　[*Exit.*]
Mos.	[*Aside.*] Bountiful bones! What horrid strange offence
	Did he commit 'gainst nature, in his youth,
	Worthy this age? — You see, sir, [*to* VOLT] how I work
	Unto your ends; take you no notice.
VOLT.	No,
	I'll leave you.
Mos.	All is yours, the devil and all,
	Good advocate! — Madam, I'll bring you home.
LADY P.	No, I'll go see your patron.
Mos.	That you shall not:
	I'll tell you why. My purpose is to urge
	My patron to reform his will, and for
	The zeal you 've shown to-day, whereas before
	You were but third or fourth, you shall be now
	Put in the first; which would appear as begg'd
	If you were present. Therefore —
LADY P.	You shall sway me. 　　　　　　[*Exeunt.*]

ACT V

Scene I. — *A room in Volpone's house*

Enter VOLPONE.

VOLP. Well, I am here, and all this brunt is past.
    I ne'er was in dislike with my disguise
    Till this fled moment: here 't was good, in private;
    But in your public, — *cavè*[1] whilst I breathe.
    'Fore God, my left leg 'gan to have the cramp.
    And I apprehended straight some power had struck me
    With a dead palsy. Well! I must be merry,
    And shake it off. A many of these fears
    Would put me into some villanous disease,
    Should they come thick upon me: I'll prevent 'em.
    Give me a bowl of lusty wine, to fright
    This humour from my heart. (*Drinks.*) Hum, hum, hum!
    'T is almost gone already; I shall conquer.
    Any device now of rare ingenious knavery,
    That would possess me with a violent laughter,
    Would make me up again. (*Drinks again.*) So, so, so, so!
    This heat is life; 't is blood by this time: — Mosca!

---

1. cavè] Latin for "beware," "watch out."

SCENE II. — *The same*

VOLPONE. *Enter* MOSCA.

MOS.   How now, sir? Does the day look clear again?
        Are we recover'd, and wrought out of error,
        Into our way, to see our path before us?
        Is our trade free once more?

VOLP.   Exquisite Mosca!

MOS.   Was it not carri'd learnedly?

VOLP.   And stoutly:
        Good wits are greatest in extremities.

MOS.   It were folly beyond thought to trust
        Any grand act unto a cowardly spirit.
        You are not taken with it enough, methinks.

VOLP.   O, more than if I had enjoy'd the wench:
        The pleasure of all woman-kind 's not like it.

MOS.   Why, now you speak, sir. We must here be fix'd;
        Here we must rest; this is our masterpiece;
        We cannot think to go beyond this.

VOLP.   True,
        Thou hast play'd thy prize, my precious Mosca.

MOS.   Nay, sir,
        To gull the court—

VOLP.   And quite divert the torrent
        Upon the innocent.

MOS.   Yes, and to make
        So rare a music out of discords—

VOLP.   Right.
        That yet to me 's the strangest, how thou 'st borne it!
        That these, being so divided 'mongst themselves,
        Should not scent somewhat, or in me or thee,
        Or doubt their own side.

MOS.   True, they will not see 't.
        Too much light blinds 'em, I think. Each of 'em
        Is so possest and stuft with his own hopes
        That anything unto the contrary,

	Never so true, or never so apparent, Never so palpable, they will resist it —
VOLP.	Like a temptation of the devil.
MOS.	Right, sir.

MOS.   Right, sir.
Merchants may talk of trade, and your great signiors
Of land that yields well; but if Italy
Have any glebe[1] more fruitful than these fellows,
I am deceiv'd. Did not your advocate rare?

VOLP. O — "My most honour'd fathers, my grave fathers,
Under correction of your fatherhoods,
What face of truth is here? If these strange deeds
May pass, most honour'd fathers" — I had much ado
To forbear laughing.

MOS.   It seem'd to me, you sweat, sir.

VOLP. In troth, I did a little.

MOS.   But confess, sir,
Were you not daunted?

VOLP.   In good faith, I was
A little in a mist, but not dejected;
Never but still myself.

MOS.   I think it, sir.
Now, so truth help me, I must needs say this, sir,
And out of conscience for your advocate,
He has taken pains, in faith, sir, and deserv'd,
In my poor judgment, I speak it under favour,
Not to contrary you, sir, very richly —
Well — to be cozen'd.

VOLP.   Troth, and I think so too,
By that I heard him in the latter end.

MOS. O, but before, sir: had you heard him first
Draw it to certain heads, then aggravate,
Then use his vehement figures — I look'd still
When he would shift a shirt;[2] and doing this
Out of pure love, no hope of gain —

VOLP.   'T is right.
I cannot answer him, Mosca, as I would,
Not yet; but for thy sake, at thy entreaty,

---

1. *glebe*] soil.
2. *shift a shirt*] change his shirt (because he had sweated so much over his speech).

	I will begin, even now — to vex 'em all,
	This very instant.
MOS.	Good sir.
VOLP.	Call the dwarf
	And eunuch forth.
MOS.	Castrone, Nano!

[*Enter* CASTRONE *and* NANO.]

NANO.	Here.
VOLP.	Shall we have a jig now?
MOS.	What you please, sir.
VOLP.	Go,
	Straight give out about the streets, you two,
	That I am dead; do it with constancy,
	Sadly,[3] do you hear? Impute it to the grief
	Of this late slander.

[*Exeunt* CAST. *and* NANO.]

MOS.	What do you mean, sir?
VOLP.	O,
	I shall have instantly my Vulture, Crow,
	Raven, come flying hither, on the news,
	To peck for carrion, my she-wolf, and all,
	Greedy, and full of expectation —
MOS.	And then to have it ravish'd from their mouths!
VOLP.	'T is true. I will ha' thee put on a gown,
	And take upon thee, as thou wert mine heir;
	Show 'em a will. Open that chest, and reach
	Forth one of those that has the blanks; I'll straight
	Put in thy name.
MOS.	It will be rare, sir.

[*Gives him a paper.*]

VOLP.	Ay,
	When they e'en gape, and find themselves deluded —
MOS.	Yes.
VOLP.	And thou use them scurvily!
	Get on thy gown.
MOS.	[*putting on a gown.*] But what, sir, if they ask
	After the body?
VOLP.	Say, it was corrupted.

3. *Sadly*] Seriously.

MOS.   I'll say it stunk, sir; and was fain to have it
       Coffin'd up instantly, and sent away.

VOLP.   Anything; what thou wilt. Hold, here's my will.
       Get thee a cap, a count-book, pen and ink,
       Papers afore thee; sit as thou wert taking
       An inventory of parcels. I'll get up
       Behind the curtain, on a stool, and hearken:
       Sometime peep over, see how they do look,
       With what degrees their blood doth leave their faces.
       O, 't will afford me a rare meal of laughter!

MOS.   [*putting on a cap, and setting out the table, &c.*] Your advocate
       will turn stark dull upon it.

VOLP.   It will take off his oratory's edge.

MOS.   But your clarissimo, old roundback, he
       Will crump you like a hog-louse, with the touch.[4]

VOLP.   And what Corvino?

MOS.   O, sir, look for him,
       To-morrow morning, with a rope and dagger,
       To visit all the streets; he must run mad,
       My lady too, that came into the court,
       To bear false witness for your worship —

VOLP.   Yes,
       And kiss'd me 'fore the fathers, when my face
       Flow'd all with oils —

MOS.   And sweat, sir. Why, your gold
       Is such another med'cine, it dries up
       All those offensive savours: it transforms
       The most deformed, and restores them lovely,
       As 't were the strange poetical girdle.[5] Jove
       Could not invent t' himself a shroud more subtle
       To pass Acrisius'[6] guards. It is the thing
       Makes all the world her grace, her youth, her beauty.

VOLP.   I think she loves me.

MOS.   Who? The lady, sir?
       She's jealous of you.

VOLP.   Dost thou say so?
                      [*Knocking within.*]

---

4. *Will crump . . . touch*] There was a kind of louse that would curl (crump) up when
touched.

5. *poetical girdle*] The girdle of Venus made any wearer irresistibly beautiful.

6. *Acrisius*] the father of Danaë, who locked her up in a tower.

Mos.	<div style="text-align:right">Hark.</div>
	There's some already.
Volp.	<div style="text-align:right">Look.</div>
Mos.	<div style="text-align:right">It is the Vulture;</div>
	He has the quickest scent.
Volp.	<div style="text-align:right">I'll to my place,</div>
	Thou to thy posture. *[Goes behind the curtain.]*
Mos.	I am set.
Volp.	<div style="text-align:right">But, Mosca,</div>
	Play the artificer now, torture 'em rarely.

SCENE III. — *The same*

MOSCA. *Enter* VOLTORE.

Volt.	How now, my Mosca?
Mos.	[*writing*]. "Turkey carpets, nine —"
Volt.	Taking an inventory! that is well.
Mos.	"Two suits of bedding, tissue —"
Volt.	Where's the will?
	Let me read that the while.

[*Enter* Servants *with* CORBACCIO *in a chair.*]

Corb.	<div style="text-align:right">So, set me down,</div>
	And get you home. *[Exeunt* Servants.]
Volt.	Is he come now, to trouble us?
Mos.	"Of cloth of gold, two more —"
Corb.	Is it done, Mosca?
Mos.	"Of several velvets, eight —"
Volt.	I like his care.
Corb.	Dost thou not hear?

[*Enter* CORVINO.]

Corv.	Ha! is the hour come, Mosca?
Volp.	Ay, now they muster.
	<div style="text-align:right">*[Peeps from behind a traverse.]*</div>
Corv.	What does the advocate here,
	Or this Corbaccio?

CORB.   What do these here?

[*Enter* LADY POL. WOULD-BE.]

LADY P.   Mosca!
         Is his thread spun?
MOS.   "Eight chests of linen —"
VOLP.   O,
         My fine Dame Would-be, too!
CORV.   Mosca, the will,
         That I may show it these, and rid 'em hence.
MOS.   "Six chests of diaper, four of damask." — There.
                    [*Gives them the will carelessly, over his shoulder.*]
CORB.   Is that the will?
MOS.   "Down-beds, and bolsters —"
VOLP.   Rare!
         Be busy still. Now they begin to flutter:
         They never think of me. Look, see, see, see!
         How their swift eyes run over the long deed,
         Unto the name, and to the legacies,
         What is bequeath'd them there —
MOS.   "Ten suits of hangings —"
VOLP.   Ay, in their garters, Mosca. Now their hopes
         Are at the gasp.
VOLT.   Mosca the heir.
CORB.   What's that?
VOLP.   My advocate is dumb; look to my merchant,
         He 's heard of some strange storm, a ship is lost,
         He faints; my lady will swoon. Old glazen-eyes,
         He hath not reach'd his despair yet.
CORB.   All these
         Are out of hope; I am, sure, the man.
                                   [*Takes the will.*]
CORV.   But, Mosca —
MOS.   "Two cabinets —"
CORV.   Is this in earnest?
MOS.   "One
         Of ebony —"
CORV.   Or do you but delude me?
MOS.   "The other, mother of pearl." — I'm very busy,

	Good faith, it is a fortune thrown upon me —
	"Item, one salt of agate" — not my seeking.
LADY P.	Do you hear, sir?
MOS.	"A perfum'd box" — Pray you forbear,
	You see I'm troubl'd — "made of an onyx —"
LADY P.	How!
MOS.	To-morrow or next day, I shall be at leisure
	To talk with you all.
CORV.	Is this my large hope's issue?
LADY P.	Sir, I must have a fairer answer.
MOS.	Madam!

Marry, and shall: pray you, fairly quit my house.
Nay, raise no tempest with your looks; but hark you,
Remember what your ladyship off'red me
To put you in an heir; go to, think on it:
And what you said e'en your best madams did
For maintenance; and why not you? Enough.
Go home, and use the poor Sir Pol, your knight, well,
For fear I tell some riddles; go, be melancholic.

                                   [*Exit* LADY WOULD-BE.]

VOLP.	O, my fine devil!
CORV.	Mosca, pray you a word.
MOS.	Lord! will not you take your dispatch hence yet?

Methinks, of all, you should have been th' example.
Why should you stay here? With what thought, what promise?
Hear you; do you not know, I know you an ass,
And that you would most fain have been a wittol[1]
If fortune would have let you? that you are
A declar'd cuckold, on good terms? This pearl,
You'll say, was yours? right: this diamond?
I'll not deny 't, but thank you. Much here else?
It may be so. Why, think that these good works
May help to hide your bad. I'll not betray you;
Although you be but extraordinary,
And have it only in title, it sufficeth:
Go home, be melancholy too, or mad.   [*Exit* CORVINO.]

| VOLP. | Rare Mosca! how his villany becomes him! |
| VOLT. | Certain he doth delude all these for me. |

---

1. *wittol*] a pimp for his own wife.

CORB.	Mosca the heir!
VOLP.	O, his four eyes have found it.
CORB.	I am cozen'd, cheated, by a parasiteslave;
	Harlot,[2] th' hast gull'd me.
MOS.	Yes, sir. Stop your mouth,

Or I shall draw the only tooth is left.
Are not you he, that filthy covetous wretch,
With the three legs, that here, in hope of prey,
Have, any time this three years, snuff'd about,
With your most grov'ling nose, and would have hir'd
Me to the pois'ning of my patron, sir?
Are not you he that have to-day in court
Profess'd the disinheriting of your son?
Perjur'd yourself? Go home, and die, and stink;
If you but croak a syllable, all comes out:
Away, and call your porters! [*Exit* CORBACCIO.] Go, go, stink.

VOLP.	Excellent varlet!
VOLT.	Now, my faithful Mosca,
	I find thy constancy —
MOS.	Sir!
VOLT.	Sincere.
MOS.	[*writing.*] "A table

Of porphyry" — I marle[3] you'll be thus troublesome.

VOLT.	Nay, leave off now, they are gone.
MOS.	Why, who are you?

What! who did send for you? O, cry you mercy,
Reverend sir! Good faith, I am griev'd for you,
That any chance of mine should thus defeat
Your (I must needs say) most deserving travails:
But I protest, sir, it was cast upon me,
And I could almost wish to be without it,
But that the will o' the dead must be observ'd.
Marry, my joy is that you need it not;
You have a gift, sir (thank your education),
Will never let you want, while there are men,
And malice, to breed causes.[4] Would I had

---

2. *Harlot*] frequently used of both sexes, here meaning "scoundrel."
3. *marle*] marvel.
4. *causes*] lawsuits.

But half the like, for all my fortune, sir!
If I have any suits, as I do hope,
Things being so easy and direct, I shall not,
I will make bold with your obstreperous aid,
Conceive me — for your fee, sir. In mean time,
You that have so much law, I know ha' the conscience
Not to be covetous of what is mine.
Good sir, I thank you for my plate; 't will help
To set up a young man. Good faith, you look
As you were costive; best go home and purge, sir.

[Exit VOLTORE.]

VOLP.   [*comes from behind the curtain.*] Bid him eat lettuce[5] well. My
           witty mischief,
      Let me embrace thee. O that I could now
      Transform thee to a Venus! — Mosca, go,
      Straight take my habit of clarissimo,[6]
      And walk the streets; be seen, torment 'em more:
      We must pursue, as well as plot. Who would
      Have lost this feast?

MOS.   I doubt it will lose them.

VOLP.   O, my recovery shall recover all.
      That I could now but think on some disguise
      To meet 'em in, and ask 'em questions:
      How I would vex 'em still at every turn!

MOS.   Sir, I can fit you.

VOLP.   Canst thou?

MOS.   Yes, I know
      One o' the commandadori, sir, so like you;
      Him will I straight make drunk, and bring you his habit.

VOLP.   A rare disguise, and answering thy brain!
      O, I will be a sharp disease unto 'em.

MOS.   Sir, you must look for curses —

VOLP.   Till they burst;
      The Fox fares ever best when he is curst.

[Exeunt.]

5. *lettuce*] thought to have a soporific effect.
6. *clarissimo*] patrician.

SCENE IV.—*A hall in Sir Politic's house*

Enter PEREGRINE *disguised and* 3 Mercatori.

PER.   Am I enough disguis'd?
1ST MER.   I warrant you.
PER.   All my ambition is to fright him only.
2ND MER.   If you could ship him away, 't were excellent.
3RD MER.   To Zant, or to Aleppo![1]
PER.   Yes, and ha' his
            Adventures put i' th' Book of Voyages,
            And his gull'd story regist'red for truth.
            Well, gentlemen, when I am in a while,
            And that you think us warm in our discourse,
            Know your approaches.
1ST MER.   Trust it to our care.
                                        [*Exeunt* Merchants.]

[*Enter* Waiting-woman.]

PER.   Save you, fair lady! Is Sir Pol within?
WOM.   I do not know, sir.
PER.   Pray you say unto him
            Here is a merchant, upon earnest business,
            Desires to speak with him.
WOM.   I will see, sir.   [*Exit.*]
PER.   Pray you.
            I see the family is all female here.

[*Re-enter* Waiting-woman.]

WOM.   He says, sir, he has weighty affairs of state,
            That now require him whole; some other time
            You may possess him.
PER.   Pray you say again,
            If those require him whole, these will exact him,

1. *Zant, Aleppo*] Zakynthos (Zant) is an Ionian island; Aleppo is in Syria.

Whereof I bring him tidings. [*Exit* Woman.] What might be
His grave affair of state now! How to make
Bolognian sausages here in Venice, sparing
One o' th' ingredients?

[*Re-enter* Waiting-woman.]

WOM.   Sir, he says, he knows
By your word "tidings," that you are no statesman,
And therefore wills you stay.
PER.   Sweet, pray you return him;
I have not read so many proclamations,
And studied them for words, as he has done —
But — here he deigns to come.   [*Exit* Woman.]

[*Enter* SIR POLITIC.]

SIR P.   Sir, I must crave
Your courteous pardon. There hath chanc'd today
Unkind disaster 'twixt my lady and me;
And I was penning my apology,
To give her satisfaction, as you came now.
PER.   Sir, I am griev'd I bring you worse disaster:
The gentleman you met at th' port to-day,
That told you he was newly arriv'd —
SIR P.   Ay, was
A fugitive punk?
PER.   No, sir, a spy set on you:
And he has made relation to the senate,
That you profest to him to have a plot
To sell the State of Venice to the Turk.
SIR P.   O me!
PER.   For which warrants are sign'd by this time
To apprehend you, and to search your study
For papers —
SIR P.   Alas, sir, I have none, but notes
Drawn out of play-books —
PER.   All the better, sir.
SIR P.   And some essays. What shall I do?
PER.   Sir, best
Convey yourself into a sugar-chest;

         Or, if you could lie round, a frail[2] were rare;
         And I could send you aboard.

SIR P.   Sir, I but talk'd so,
         For discourse sake merely.   [*They knock without.*]

PER.   Hark! they are there.

SIR P.   I am a wretch, a wretch!

PER.   What will you do, sir?
         Have you ne'er a currant-butt[3] to leap into?
         They'll put you to the rack; you must be sudden.

SIR P.   Sir, I have an engine[4] —

3RD MER.   [*within.*]   Sir Politic Would-be!

2ND MER.   [*within.*] Where is he?

SIR P.   That I've thought upon before time.

PER.   What is it?

SIR P.   I shall ne'er endure the torture.
         Marry, it is, sir, of a tortoise-shell,
         Fitted for these extremities: pray you, sir, help me.
         Here I've a place, sir, to put back my legs,
         Please you to lay it on, sir, [*Lies down while* PER. *places the*
            shell upon him.]—with this cap,
         And my black gloves. I'll lie, sir, like a tortoise,
         Till they are gone.

PER.   And call you this an engine?

SIR P.   Mine own device.—Good sir, bid my wife's women
         To burn my papers.   [*Exit* PER.]

The three Merchants *rush in.*

1ST MER.   Where is he hid?

3RD MER.   We must,
         And will sure find him.

2ND MER.   Which is his study?

[*Re-enter* PEREGRINE.]

1ST MER.   What
         Are you, sir?

PER.   I'm a merchant, that came here
         To look upon this tortoise.

---

2. *frail*] rush basket.
3. *currant-butt*] cask for holding currants.
4. *engine*] contrivance.

3RD MER.   How!
1ST MER.   St. Mark!
        What beast is this?
PER.   It is a fish.
2ND MER.   Come out here!
PER.   Nay, you may strike him, sir, and tread upon him;
        He'll bear a cart.
1ST MER.   What, to run over him?
PER.   Yes, sir.
3RD MER.   Let's jump upon him.
2ND MER.   Can he not go?
PER.   He creeps, sir.
1ST MER.   Let's see him creep.
PER.   No, good sir, you will hurt him.
2ND MER.   Heart, I will see him creep, or prick his guts.
3RD MER.   Come out here!
PER.   Pray you, sir, creep a little.
1ST MER.   Forth.
2ND MER.   Yet further.
PER.   Good sir! — Creep.
2ND MER.   We'll see his legs.
        [*They pull off the shell and discover him.*]
3RD MER.   Gods so, he has garters!
1ST MER.   Ay, and gloves!
2ND MER.   Is this
        Your fearful tortoise?
PER.   [*discovering himself.*] Now, Sir Pol, we're even;
        For your next project I shall be prepar'd:
        I am sorry for the funeral of your notes, sir.
1ST MER.   'T were a rare motion[5] to be seen in Fleet-street.
2ND MER.   Ay, in the Term.
1ST MER.   Or Smithfield, in the fair.
3RD MER.   Methinks 't is but a melancholic sight.
PER.   Farewell, most politic tortoise!
                                [*Exeunt* PER. *and* Merchants.]

[*Re-enter* Waiting-woman.]

SIR P.   Where's my lady?
        Knows she of this?

        5. *motion*] show.

WOM.   I know not, sir.
SIR P.   Enquire. —
              O, I shall be the fable of all feasts,
              The freight of the gazetti,[6] ship-boys' tale;
              And, which is worst, even talk for ordinaries.
WOM.   My lady's come most melancholic home,
              And says, sir, she will straight to sea, for physic.
SIR P.   And I, to shun this place and clime for ever,
              Creeping with house on back, and think it well
              To shrink my poor head in my politic shell.

                                                              [*Exeunt.*]

              SCENE V. — *A room in Volpone's house*

Enter MOSCA *in the habit of a clarissimo, and* VOLPONE *in that of a
commandadore.*

VOLP.   Am I then like him?
MOS.   O, sir, you are he;
              No man can sever you.
VOLP.   Good.
MOS.   But what am I?
VOLP.   'Fore heaven, a brave clarissimo; thou becom'st it!
              Pity thou wert not born one.
MOS.   [*Aside.*]   If I hold
              My made one, 't will be well.
VOLP.   I'll go and see
              What news first at the court.   [*Exit.*]
MOS.   Do so. My Fox
              Is out of his hole, and ere he shall re-enter,
              I'll make him languish in his borrow'd case,[1]
              Except he come to composition with me. —
              Androgyno, Castrone, Nano!

---

6. *The freight of the gazetti*] The theme of the newspapers.

---

1. *his borrow'd case*] his disguise.

[*Enter* ANDROGYNO, CASTRONE, *and* NANO.]

ALL.   Here.
MOS.   Go, recreate yourselves abroad; go, sport. —   [*Exeunt.*]
          So, now I have the keys, and am possest.
          Since he will needs be dead afore his time,
          I'll bury him, or gain by 'm: I'm his heir,
          And so will keep me, till he share at least.
          To cozen him of all, were but a cheat
          Well plac'd; no man would construe it a sin:
          Let his sport pay for 't. This is call'd the Fox-trap.   [*Exit.*]

SCENE VI. — *A street*

Enter CORBACCIO, CORVINO.

CORB.   They say the court is set.
CORV.   We must maintain
          Our first tale good, for both our reputations.
CORB.   Why, mine's no tale: my son would there have kill'd me.
CORV.   That's true, I had forgot: — mine is, I'm sure.
          But for your will, sir.
CORB.   Ay, I'll come upon him
          For that hereafter, now his patron's dead.

[*Enter* VOLPONE.]

VOLP.   Signior Corvino! and Corbaccio! sir,
          Much joy unto you.
CORV.   Of what?
VOLP.   The sudden good
          Dropt down upon you—
CORB.   Where?
VOLP.   And none knows how,
          From old Volpone, sir.
CORB.   Out, arrant knave!
VOLP.   Let not your too much wealth, sir, make you furious.
CORB.   Away, thou varlet.
VOLP.   Why, sir?
CORB.   Dost thou mock me?

VOLP.   You mock the world, sir; did you not change wills?
CORB.   Out, harlot!
VOLP.   O! belike you are the man,
         Signior Corvino? Faith, you carry it well;
         You grow not mad withal; I love your spirit:
         You are not over-leaven'd with your fortune.
         You should ha' some would swell now, like a wine-fat,
         With such an autumn. — Did he gi' you all, sir?
CORB.   Avoid, you rascal!
VOLP.   Troth, your wife has shown
         Herself a very woman; but you are well,
         You need not care, you have a good estate,
         To bear it out, sir, better by this chance:
         Except Corbaccio have a share.
CORB.   Hence, varlet.
VOLP.   You will not be acknown, sir; why, 't is wise.
         Thus do all gamesters, at all games, dissemble:
         No man will seem to win. [*Exeunt* CORVINO *and* CORBAC-
            CIO.] Here comes my vulture,
         Heaving his beak up i' the air, and snuffing.

SCENE VII. — *The same*

VOLPONE. *Enter* VOLTORE.

VOLT.   Outstrip thus, by a parasite! a slave,
         Would run on errands, and make legs for crumbs!
         Well, what I'll do —
VOLP.   The court stays for your worship.
         I e'en rejoice, sir, at your worship's happiness,
         And that it fell into so learned hands,
         That understand the fing'ring —
VOLT.   What do you mean?
VOLP.   I mean to be a suitor to your worship,
         For the small tenement, out of reparations,[1]
         That, at the end of your long row of houses, ·

---

1. *out of reparations*] out of repair.

By the Piscaria: it was, in Volpone's time,
Your predecessor, ere he grew diseas'd,
A handsome, pretty, custom'd[2] bawdy-house
As any was in Venice, none disprais'd;
But fell with him: his body and that house
Decay'd together.

VOLT.   Come, sir, leave your prating.

VOLP.   Why, if your worship give me but your hand
That I may ha' the refusal, I have done.
'T is a mere toy to you, sir; candle-rents;[3]
As your learn'd worship knows —

VOLT.   What do I know?

VOLP.   Marry, no end of your wealth, sir; God decrease it!

VOLT.   Mistaking knave! what, mock'st thou my misfortune? [*Exit.*]

VOLP.   His blessing on your heart, sir; would 't were more! —
Now to my first again, at the next corner.

                                        [*Exit.*]

SCENE VIII. — *The Scrutineo*

Enter CORBACCIO *and* CORVINO; — (MOSCA *passant.*)

CORB.   See, in our habit![1] see the impudent varlet!

CORV.   That I could shoot mine eyes at him, like gun-stones!

[*Enter* VOLPONE.]

VOLP.   But is this true, sir, of the parasite?

CORB.   Again, t' afflict us! monster!

VOLP.   In good faith, sir,
I'm heartily griev'd, a beard of your grave length
Should be so over-reach'd. I never brook'd
That parasite's hair; methought his nose should cozen:[2]

---

2. *custom'd*] well-frequented.
3. *candle-rents*] trivial things (to a rich man).

---

1. *in our habit*] dressed like us.
2. *cozen*] swindle.

There still was somewhat in his look, did promise
The bane of a clarissimo.

CORB.   Knave —

VOLP.   Methinks
Yet you, that are so traded i' the world,
A witty merchant, the fine bird, Corvino,
That have such moral emblems on your name,
Should not have sung your shame, and dropt your cheese,
To let the Fox laugh at your emptiness.

CORV.   Sirrah, you think the privilege of the place,
And your red saucy cap, that seems to me
Nail'd to your jolt-head with those two chequins,
Can warrant your abuses; come you hither:
You shall perceive, sir, I dare beat you; approach.

VOLP.   No haste, sir, I do know your valour well,
Since you durst publish what you are, sir.

CORV.   Tarry,
I'd speak with you.

VOLP.   Sir, sir, another time —

CORV.   Nay, now.

VOLP.   O lord, sir! I were a wise man,
Would stand the fury of a distracted cuckold.
                              [MOSCA *walks by them.*]

CORB.   What, come again!

VOLP.   Upon 'em, Mosca; save me.

CORB.   The air's infected where he breathes.

CORV.   Let's fly him.
                              [*Exeunt* CORV. *and* CORB.]

VOLP.   Excellent basilisk! turn upon the vulture.

SCENE IX. — *The same*

MOSCA, VOLPONE. [*Enter*] VOLTORE.

VOLT.   Well, flesh-fly, it is summer with you now;
Your winter will come on.

MOS.   Good advocate,
Prithee not rail, nor threaten out of place thus;

  Thou 'lt make a solecism, as madam says.
  Get you a biggin[1] more; your brain breaks loose.   [*Exit.*]
VOLT. Well sir.
VOLP. Would you ha' me beat the insolent slave,
  Throw dirt upon his first good clothes?
VOLT.   This same
  Is doubtless some familiar.
VOLP.   Sir, the court,
  In troth, stays for you. I am mad, a mule
  That never read Justinian, should get up,
  And ride an advocate. Had you no quirk
  To avoid gullage, sir, by such a creature?
  I hope you do but jest; he has not done 't:
  This 's but confederacy to blind the rest.
  You are the heir?
VOLT.   A strange, officious,
  Troublesome knave! thou dost torment me.
VOLP.   I know—
  It cannot be, sir, that you should be cozen'd;
  'T is not within the wit of man to do it;
  You are so wise, so prudent; and 't is fit
  That wealth and wisdom still should go together. [*Exeunt.*]

SCENE X. — *The same*

Enter 4 Avocatori, Notario, BONARIO, CELIA, CORBACCIO, CORVINO,
Commandadori, [*Saffi, etc.*]

1ST AVOC. Are all the parties here?
NOT.   All but th' advocate.
2ND AVOC. And here he comes.

[*Enter* VOLTORE *and* VOLPONE.]

1ST AVOC. Then bring them forth to sentence.
VOLT.   O, my most honour'd fathers, let your mercy
    Once win upon your justice, to forgive —
    I am distracted —

 1. *biggin*] barrister's cap.

VOLP.   (*Aside*.) What will he do now?
VOLT.   O,
    I know not which t' address myself to first;
    Whether your fatherhoods, or these innocents —
CORV.   (*Aside*.) Will he betray himself?
VOLT.   Whom equally
    I have abus'd, out of most covetous ends —
CORV.   The man is mad!
CORB.   What's that?
CORV.   He is possest.
VOLT.   For which, now struck in conscience, here I prostrate
    Myself at your offended feet, for pardon.
1ST, 2ND AVOC.   Arise.
CEL.   O heaven, how just thou art!
VOLP.   I'm caught
    I' mine own noose —
CORV.   [*to* CORBACCIO.] Be constant, sir; nought now
    Can help but impudence.
1ST AVOC.   Speak forward.
COM.   Silence!
VOLT.   It is not passion in me, reverend fathers,
    But only conscience, conscience, my good sires,
    That makes me now tell truth. That parasite,
    That knave, hath been the instrument of all.
1ST AVOC.   Where is that knave? Fetch him.
VOLP.   I go.   [*Exit.*]
CORV.   Grave fathers,
    This man 's distracted; he confest it now:
    For, hoping to be old Volpone's heir,
    Who now is dead —
3RD AVOC.   How!
2ND AVOC.   Is Volpone dead?
CORV.   Dead since, grave fathers.
BON.   O sure vengeance!
1ST AVOC.   Stay,
    Then he was no deceiver?
VOLT.   O no, none:
    This parasite, grave fathers.
CORV.   He does speak
    Out of mere envy, 'cause the servant 's made
    The thing he gap'd for. Please your fatherhoods,

This is the truth, though I'll not justify
The other, but he may be some-deal faulty.

VOLT. Ay, to your hopes, as well as mine, Corvino:
But I'll use modesty.[1] Pleaseth your wisdoms,
To view these certain notes, and but confer[2] them;
And as I hope favour, they shall speak clear truth.

CORV. The devil has ent'red him!

BON. Or bides in you.

4TH AVOC. We have done ill, by a public officer
To send for him, if he be heir.

2ND AVOC. For whom?

4TH AVOC. Him that they call the parasite.

3RD AVOC. 'T is true,
He is a man of great estate, now left.

4TH AVOC. Go you, and learn his name, and say the court
Entreats his presence here, but to the clearing
Of some few doubts. [*Exit* Notary.]

2ND AVOC. This same 's a labyrinth!

1ST AVOC. Stand you unto your first report?

CORV. My state,
My life, my fame —

BON. Where is 't?

CORV. Are at the stake.

1ST AVOC. Is yours so too?

CORB. The advocate 's a knave,
And has a forked tongue —

2ND AVOC. Speak to the point.

CORB. So is the parasite too.

1ST AVOC. This is confusion.

VOLT. I do beseech your fatherhoods, read but those —
[*Giving them papers.*]

CORV. And credit nothing the false spirit hath writ:
It cannot be but he's possest, grave fathers.
[*The scene closes.*]

---

1. *modesty*] moderation.
2. *confer*] compare.

Scene XI. — A *street*

Enter VOLPONE.

VOLP.   To make a snare for mine own neck! and run
              My head into it, wilfully! with laughter!
              When I had newly scap'd, was free and clear,
              Out of mere wantonness! O, the dull devil
              Was in this brain of mine when I devis'd it,
              And Mosca gave it second; he must now
              Help to sear up this vein, or we bleed dead.

[*Enter* NANO, ANDROGYNO, *and* CASTRONE.]

              How now! Who let you loose? Whither go you now?
              What, to buy gingerbread, or to drown kitlings?
NAN.   Sir, Master Mosca call'd us out of doors,
              And bid us all go play, and took the keys.
AND.   Yes.
VOLP.   Did Master Mosca take the keys? Why, so!
              I'm farther in. These are my fine conceits!
              I must be merry, with a mischief to me!
              What a vile wretch was I, that could not bear
              My fortune soberly? I must ha' my crochets,[1]
              And my conundrums! Well, go you, and seek him:
              His meaning may be truer than my fear.
              Bid him, he straight come to me to the court;
              Thither will I, and, if 't be possible,
              Unscrew my advocate, upon new hopes:
              When I provok'd him, then I lost myself.

                                                       [*Exeunt.*]

---

1. *crochets*] perverse conceits, odd fancies.

SCENE XII. — *The Scrutineo*

Avocatori, BONARIO, CELIA, CORBACCIO, CORVINO, Commandadori,
Saffi, *etc., as before.*

1ST AVOC. These things can ne'er be reconcil'd.
           He here   [*showing the papers*]
           Professeth that the gentleman was wrong'd,
           And that the gentlewoman was brought thither,
           Forc'd by her husband, and there left.
VOLT.   Most true.
CEL.   How ready is heaven to those that pray!
1ST AVOC.   But that
           Volpone would have ravish'd her, he holds
           Utterly false, knowing his impotence.
CORV.   Grave fathers, he's possest; again, I say,
           Possest: nay, if there be possession, and
           Obsession, he has both.
3RD AVOC.   Here comes our officer.

[*Enter* VOLPONE.]

VOLP.   The parasite will straight be here, grave fathers.
4TH AVOC. You might invent some other name, sir varlet.
3RD AVOC. Did not the notary meet him?
VOLP.   Not that I know.
4TH AVOC. His coming will clear all.
2ND AVOC.   Yet it is misty.
VOLT.   May 't please your fatherhoods —
VOLP.   (*whispers* VOLT.)   Sir, the parasite
           Will'd me to tell you that his master lives;
           That you are still the man; your hopes the same;
           And this was only a jest —
VOLT.   How?
VOLP.   Sir, to try
           If you were firm, and how you stood affected.
VOLT.   Art sure he lives?
VOLP.   Do I live, sir?

VOLT.   O me!
    I was too violent.
VOLP.   Sir, you may redeem it.
    They said you were possest; fall down, and seem so:
    I'll help to make it good. (VOLTORE *falls*.) God bless the
       man! —
    Stop your wind hard, and swell — See, see, see, see!
    He vomits crooked pins! His eyes are set,
    Like a dead hare's hung in a poulter's shop!
    His mouth's running away! Do you see, signior?
    Now it is in his belly.
CORV.   Ay, the devil!
VOLP.   Now in his throat.
CORV.   Ay, I perceive it plain.
VOLP.   'T will out, 't will out! stand clear. See where it flies,
    In shape of a blue toad, with a bat's wings!
    Do you not see it, sir?
CORB.   What? I think I do.
CORV.   'T is too manifest.
VOLP.   Look! he comes t' himself!
VOLT.   Where am I?
VOLP.   Take good heart, the worst is past, sir.
    You're dispossest.
1ST AVOC.   What accident is this!
2ND AVOC. Sudden and full of wonder!
3RD AVOC.   If he were
    Possest, as it appears, all this is nothing.
CORV.   He has been often subject to these fits.
1ST AVOC.   Show him that writing: — do you know it, sir?
VOLP.   (*whispers* VOLT.) Deny it, sir, forswear it; know it not.
VOLT.   Yes, I do know it well, it is my hand;
    But all that it contains is false.
BON.   O practice![1]
2ND AVOC. What maze is this!
1ST AVOC.   Is he not guilty then,
    Whom you there name the parsite?
VOLT.   Grave fathers,
    No more than his good patron, old Volpone.

---

1. *practice*] conspiracy.

4TH AVOC. Why, he is dead.
VOLT.   O no, my honour'd fathers,
        He lives —
1ST AVOC. How! lives?
VOLT.   Lives.
2ND AVOC.   This is subtler yet!
3RD AVOC. You said he was dead.
VOLT.   Never.
3RD AVOC.   You said so.
CORV.   I heard so.
4TH AVOC. Here comes the gentleman; make him way.

[*Enter* MOSCA.]

3RD AVOC.   A stool,
4TH AVOC. [*Aside.*] A proper man; and were Volpone dead,
        A fit match for my daughter.
3RD AVOC.   Give him way.
VOLP.   [*Aside to* MOS.] Mosca, I was a'most lost; the advocate
        Had betray'd all; but now it is recover'd;
        All's on the hinge again — Say I am living.
MOS.   What busy knave is this! — Most reverend fathers,
        I sooner had attended your grave pleasures,
        But that my order for the funeral
        Of my dear patron did require me —
VOLP.   [*Aside.*]   Mosca!
MOS.   Whom I intend to bury like a gentleman.
VOLP.   [*Aside.*] Ay, quick, and cozen me of all.
2ND AVOC.   Still stranger!
        More intricate!
1ST AVOC.   And come about again!
4TH AVOC. [*Aside.*] It is a match, my daughter is bestow'd.
MOS.   [*Aside to* VOLP.] Will you gi' me half?
VOLP.   First I'll be hang'd.
MOS.   I know
        Your voice is good, cry not so loud.
1ST AVOC.   Demand
        The advocate. — Sir, did you not affirm
        Volpone was alive?
VOLP.   Yes, and he is;

| | This gent'man told me so. — [*Aside to* MOS.] Thou shalt have half. |

MOS.   Whose drunkard is this same? Speak, some that know him:
  I never saw his face. — [*Aside to* VOLP.] I cannot now
  Afford it you so cheap.

VOLP.   No!

1ST AVOC.   What say you?

VOLT.   The officer told me.

VOLP.   I did, grave fathers,
  And will maintain he lives, with mine own life,
  And that this creature [*points to* MOS.] told me. [*Aside.*] — I
   was born
  With all good stars my enemies.

MOS.   Most grave fathers,
  If such an insolence as this must pass
  Upon me, I am silent: 't was not this
  For which you sent, I hope.

2ND AVOC.   Take him away.

VOLP.   Mosca!

3RD AVOC. Let him be whipt.

VOLP.   Wilt thou betray me?
  Cozen me?

3RD AVOC.   And taught to bear himself
   Toward a person of his rank.

4TH AVOC.   Away.
          [*The* Officers *seize* VOLPONE.]

MOS.   I humbly thank your fatherhoods.

VOLP.   Soft, soft: [*Aside.*] Whipt!
  And lose all that I have! If I confess,
  It cannot be much more.

4TH AVOC.   Sir, are you married?

VOLP.   They 'll be alli'd anon; I must be resolute;
  The Fox shall here uncase.

           Puts off his disguise.

MOS.   Patron!

VOLP.   Nay, now
  My ruin shall not come alone; your match
  I'll hinder sure: my substance shall not glue you,
  Nor screw you into a family.

Mos.	Why, patron!
Volp.	I am Volpone, and this is my knave;

[Pointing to Mosca.*]*

This [*to* Volt.], his own knave; this [*to* Corb.], avarice's
    fool;
This [*to* Corv.], a chimera of wittol, fool, and knave:
And, reverend fathers, since we all can hope
Nought but a sentence, let 's not now despair it.
You hear me brief.

Corv.	May it please your fatherhoods —
Com.	Silence.
1st Avoc.	The knot is now undone by miracle.
2nd Avoc.	Nothing can be more clear.
3rd Avoc.	Or can more prove

    These innocent.

1st Avoc.	Give 'em their liberty.
Bon.	Heaven could not long let such gross crimes be hid.
2nd Avoc.	If this be held the highway to get riches,

    May I be poor!

3rd Avoc.	This 's not the gain, but torment.
1st Avoc.	These possess wealth, as sick men possess fevers,

    Which trulier may be said to possess them.

2nd Avoc.	Disrobe that parasite.
Corv. Mos.	Most honour'd fathers —
1st Avoc.	Can you plead aught to stay the course of justice?

    If you can, speak.

Corv. Volt.	We beg favour.
Cel.	And mercy.
1st Avoc.	You hurt your innocence, suing for the guilty.

    Stand forth; and first the parasite. You appear
    T' have been the chiefest minister, if not plotter,
    In all these lewd impostures, and now, lastly,
    Have with your impudence abus'd the court,
    And habit of a gentleman of Venice,
    Being a fellow of no birth or blood:
    For which our sentence is, first, thou be whipt;
    Then live perpetual prisoner in our galleys.

Volp.	I thank you for him.
Mos.	Bane to thy wolfish nature!

1ST AVOC.   Deliver him to the saffi. [MOSCA *is carried out.*] Thou,
    Volpone,
    By blood and rank a gentleman, canst not fall
    Under like censure; but our judgment on thee
    Is, that thy substance all be straight confiscate
    To the hospital of the Incurabili:
    And since the most was gotten by imposture,
    By feigning lame, gout, palsy, and such diseases,
    Thou art to lie in prison, cramp'd with irons,
    Till thou be'st sick and lame indeed. Remove him.
          [*He is taken from the Bar.*]
VOLP.   This is called mortifying of a Fox.
1ST AVOC.   Thou, Voltore, to take away the scandal
    Thou hast giv'n all worthy men of thy profession,
    Art banish'd from their fellowship, and our state.
    Corbaccio! — bring him near. We here possess
    Thy son of all thy state, and confine thee
    To the monastery of San Spirito;
    Where, since thou knew'st not how to live well here,
    Thou shalt be learn'd to die well.
CORB.   Ha! what said he?
COM.   You shall know anon, sir.
1ST AVOC.   Thou, Corvino, shalt
    Be straight embark'd from thine own house, and row'd
    Round about Venice, through the Grand Canal,
    Wearing a cap, with fair long ass's ears,
    Instead of horns! and so to mount, a paper
    Pinn'd on thy breast, to the Berlina.[2]
CORV.   Yes,
    And have mine eyes beat out with stinking fish,
    Bruis'd fruit, and rotten eggs — 't is well. I'm glad
    I shall not see my shame yet.
1ST AVOC.   And to expiate
    Thy wrongs done to thy wife, thou art to send her
    Home to her father, with her dowry trebled:
    And these are all your judgments.
ALL.   Honour'd fathers —

 2. *Berlina*] pillory.

1ST AVOC.   Which may not be revok'd. Now you begin,
          When crimes are done and past, and to be punish'd,
          To think what your crimes are. Away with them!
          Let all that see these vices thus rewarded,
          Take heart, and love to study 'em. Mischiefs feed
          Like beasts, till they be fat, and then they bleed. [*Exeunt.*]

VOLPONE [*comes forward*].

      "The seasoning of a play is the applause.
      Now, though the Fox be punish'd by the laws,
      He yet doth hope, there is no suff'ring due,
      For any fact[3] which he hath done 'gainst you;
      If there be, censure him; here he doubtful stands:
      If not, fare jovially, and clap your hands."

                         [*Exit.*]

3. *fact*] deed.